Life and Culture
in
Ancient Indian Ashramas and Hermitages

By

Dr. R.K. Vats

Foreword by

Dr. Ravi Prakash Arya

Amazon Books, USA

In association with

INDIAN FOUNDATION FOR VEDIC SCIENCE

H.O.1051, Sector-1, Rohtak, Haryana, India Ph. +91 1262 292580
Delhi Contact Ph. Nos.: +911165188114; +91 9313033917
Emails: vedicscience@rediffmail.com
vedicscience@hotmail.com
Website : www.vedascience.com

First Edition

Kali era: 5016 (c. 2015)
Kalpa era: 1,97,29,49,116
Brahma era:15,50,21,97,9,49,116

ISBN No. 81-87710-55-1

Table of Contents

Foreword

Aśramas were the sear of learning in Ancient India. They were the centres of culture, philosophy, spirituality, education, and all types of sciences. They were headed by some high profile seer.

The students used to come to Aśramas from far and wide to educate themselves different sciences. Aśrama educated students used to set standards in the society. They used to be view makers and ideal persons in society. As such one may presume that society in ancient India was governed by Aśramas or hermitages. Sometimes it is assumed that hermitages were the places of doing penances, but the reality was quite different.

It is an urgent need of the hour that rational and scientific studies are carried out on the life and culture of ancient Indian Aśramas. Dr. R.K. Vatsa dared to take up this untouched issue and made a great break through in one of the obscured aspect of study. His studies have made it clear that Aśramas in ancient India were the seat of learning just like the modern universities. The teachers and students used to lead a very simple and austre life. That is why, the seats of learning were called Aśramas. The aśramites excercised lot of śrama (penances) in gaining and imparting the metaphysical and physical knowledge. The training given in spiritual methods in Aśramas made students eligible to be an ideal social and human beings in society. They used to be asset for the society.

There was no state funding available to Aśrama, rather they were run by society. In other words education and educational institutions were not the state liability, rather the liability of society. During post Vedic period Aśramas were known by the name Gurukulas. Till the advent of British in 18th century, there were more than 7 lakhs villages in India and every village had one Gurukula. Some of the big villages had more than two Gurukulas. This proves beyond an iota of doubt that education was given utmost priority by the state as well as society and education was not the state subject, but the responsibility of society. Till 1825, there were few schools in Britain and Europe. Only the students belonging to royalty were allowed to gain school education. But in India the statistics of atleast one Gurukula in every village shows that there was one school for 200 students and every body was allowed to gain education.

Thus, if we are able to understand the culture and functioning of Aśramas of ancient India, we would be able to understand the real picture of society in ancient India.

Principal (Dr.) Ravi Prakash Arya
114, Akash, DRDO Complex,
Lucknow Road, Timarpur, Delhi-110054
Mob. 00 91 9313033917
Email: vedicscience@hotmail.com
web: www.vedicscience.com

CHAPTER – I

INTRODUCTION

No institution of ancient India has so characteristically represented the ethos of Indian culture as the *Āśramas* or *Tapovanas*. The Ṛṣis who headed the *Āśramas* (hermitages), practically set the course of Indian culture in motion which rejuvenated it from time to time and saturated Indian life with spiritualism. The hermitages had unlimited potentiality and marvelous adaptability. Their utility has been demonstrated not only in the religious and spiritual areas but also in the secular aspects of life which were harnessed and transformed by the value system and the intellectual activity of these institutions. It is this humanizing influence of the hermitages that helped formulating the Indian view of life. Any approach to the history of India has to adopt the scale of values cultivated in the hermitages to appraise her culture and civilization. The wars and conquests, rise and fall of empires, the wealth and prosperity, the monumental activities and the traumatic political events make little appeal to the Indian mind. The holy sages and the Ṛṣis who embody spirituality at its finest, represent the true genious of India and make the greatest appeal to the Indian masses even today. Radha Krishnan[1] has rightly pointed out that "spiritual life is the

1. Introduced by Dr. Sarvepalli Radha Krishnan, (1958), *The Cultural Heritage of India*, I Ed., Calcutta, p. xxiii

genious of hermitages in India". It is no wonder, therefore, that the life and lessons of the hermitages caught the imagination of all great writers of ancient India in particular and modern India in general.

Little research work has been done that deals with the hermitages in ancient India directly and comprehensively. What has generally been attempted so far is the study of spiritualism or the ancient education. The important studies on ancient Indian education are those of A. S. Altekar[1], V.P. Bokil[2], Chinmoy Chatterjee[3], S.K. Das[4], Veda Mitra[5], R.K. Mookerji[6], S.C. Sarkar[7], F.E. Keay[8] etc. These works mainly deal with education in ancient India as a whole. The works which deal with the ancient hermitages directly are few. The significant among those are the *Āśramas-Past and Present* by P. Chenchiah and others[9] and the *Gurukula System of Education in India and its Application to Modern Times* by B. Sharan.[10] The former work contains only general account of *Āśrāmas* in

---

1 Altekar, A.S., (1957), *Education in Ancient India*, Banaras

2 Bokhil, V.P., (1925), *The History of Education in India*, Part I.

3 Chatterjee, Chinmoy, *Vedantic Education*, Lucknow.

4 Das, S.K., (1930), *The Educational System of the Ancient Hindus*, Calcutta.

5 Veda Mitra, (1964), *Education in Ancient India*, New Delhi.

6 Mookerji, R.K., (1947), *Ancient Indian Education*, London.

7 Sarkar, S.C., (1928), *Educational Ideas and Institutions in Ancient India.*

8 Keay, F.E., (1980), *Ancient Indian Education,* New Delhi.

9 Chenchiah, P. et. al., *Āśramas Past and Present*, Madras.

10 Sharan, B., (1968), *The Gurukula System of Education in India and Its Application to Modern Times*, Varanasi.

ancient literature and the nature of these instititutions. It lacks the historical perspective relating to the evolution and transformation of the hermitages in time and space and gives no critical assessment of the contribution of the hermitages to Indian society. The later work deals with the educational system of the *Gurukulas* or hermitages broadly. There has been a general tendency among scholars to give an idealized description of these institutions instead of examining their growth and development historically. G. C. Pande[1] in his comprehensive study of the origin of Buddhism investigated the origin of asceticism. But it is only partly related to our topic. He has traced the references to ascetic mode of life in literature and has not explained the origin of the phenomenon.

The scattered references to the hermitages in the ancient literature and their nostalgic description by the modern scholars do not give us an objective and comprehensive picture of the nature of these institutions and their functions. Carr has rightly pointed out, "The function of the historian is neither to love the past nor to emancipate himself from the past but to master and understand it as the key to the understanding of the present".[2] He further observes, "To love the past may easily be an expression of the nostalgic romanticism of old men and old societies, a symptom of loss of faith and interest in the present or future."[3] What is needed is, therefore, to examine the

---

1 Pande, G.C., (1974), *The Origin of Buddhism*, Delhi.

2 Carr, E.H., (1977), *What is History*, London, p.26.

problem of the hermitages in ancient India in its various aspects with regard to their nature and character, their origin and development and their role in the ancient Indian society. These historical questions about the ancient hermitages have to a large extent remained unexplored so far. The main sources for the study of the hermitages in ancient India are the literary works, composed in Sanskrit and Pali languages dealing with Vedic, post-Vedic and Buddhist philosophy. But the Vedic and post-Vedic literature is particularly important from the point of view of this study.

The prominent Vedic works are *Vedic Saṁhitās*, *Brāhmaṇas*, *Āraṇyakas* and the *Upaniṣads*. The *Saṁhitās* deal with various types of knowledge system pertaining to creation. The *Brāhmaṇas* seek to elucidate the notion of the *Saṁhitās*. The *Āraṇyakas* represent the last books of the *Brāhmaṇas* and deal with the spiritual aspect of knowledge. The *Upaniṣads* which constitute the final products of the Vedic literature constitute the secret doctrines relating to philosophical aspect of evolution of universe, men and their relations.

They contain the oldest Indian philosophy and doctrines which were explicitly developed in the later ages. Among a large number of *Upaniṣads* only those which have been commented upon by Śaṅkara are considered as main Upaniṣads and belong to the later Vedic age. The

[3] *Ibid.*,p.25.

Āraṇyakas and the *Upaniṣads* constitute the *Jñāna-Kāṇda* of the Vedas, while the *Brāhmaṇas* represent the *Karma-Kāṇda.* The *Sūtra* literature is also considered to be connected with the Vedas as their ancillary sciences. These are related to social, political and economic norms, household ceremonies and the rituals.

Although the Vedic literature does not deal directly with the hermitages, it records the names of Ṛṣis and sages which are found associated with the hermitages in the Epics and the later literature. It is an important source for tracing the origin and development of the various strands of the culture of hermitages.

The Epic literature – *Rāmāyaṇa* and the *Mahābhārata* – are the most popular in the *Sanskrit* literature. They have, in fact, served as treasure houses by the later classical writers. They represent the most important source for the study of the hermitages in ancient India. It appears that the culture of the hermitages for all practical purposes belonged to the age of the Epics. Although the said works are not the products of any single author or period, the evidence contained in these about the hermitages relates to the pre-Buddha times, i.e. at least 5000 years ago. *Mahābhārata* has been dated between 3076 BC to 3138 BC.

The *Purāṇas* also contain references to the hermitages. These are 18 in number and range over a vast period of time. The early *Purāṇas* which date to the Gupta period (327 BC to 82 BC) include, the *Markaṇḍeya*, *Matsya*, *Bhāgavata*, *Vāyu*, *Viṣṇu*, *Brahmāṇḍa* etc.

The Buddhist literature is composed in Pali and Sanskrit languages. The Pali cannon is divided into three *Piṭakas- Vinaya Piṭaka*, *Sutta Piṭaka* and the *Abhidamma Piṭ aka.* The Jatakas deal with the stories related to the previous birth of the Buddha. The Buddhist literature has been dated between C. 5th and 3rd century B.C.[1]

The Buddhist literature throws only indirect and immediate light on the hermitages in ancient India. They rather contain greater details about the life in the Buddhist Viharas and the institution of mendicancy which represent a stage later than and more advanced than that of the hermitages known from the Brahmanical literature. A corresponding Brahmanical institution was that of *Sannyāsa* which too was a later development, perhaps consequent to the challenges posed by Buddhism and Jainism to the Vedic culture. It is for this reason that the Buddhist and Jain literature has not been included in the study.

The Classical Sanskrit literature which throws useful light on hermitages includes the work of Kālidāsa, Bāṇa, Bhavabhūti, Bhāsa etc. Kālidāsa has been dated to 12th Century B.C.[2], while Bana belongs to the C. 625 A.D.[3]

---

1 Pande, G.C., (1974), *op.cit.*, Delhi, p.16.

2 Dr. Ravi Prakash Arya, 1999.

3 Altekar, A.S., (1957), op.cit.,pp.332-34.

Bhasa is placed in the century B.C.[1] and Bhavabhuti belonged to C.725 A.D.[2]

The main period of the hermitages seems to have passed away about the Gupta age (327 B.C. to 82 B.C.) when several important universities and educational institutions had grown into prominence. It is for this reason that the topic has been confined to C. 300 B.C.

In the study of the hermitages we have collected the data mainly from Vedic and post-Vedic Sanskrit literature though the Buddhist literature has also been reffered to support the evidence from Vedic literature. The evidence has been classified in the light of the geographical factors to understand the distribution of the hermitages in time[3] and space[4] and to understand their relationship with ecology. The functional classification[5] helped to work out the chief aspects of the life in the hermitages. The details of the life pattern of the hermitages has been analysed to throw light on the various aspects, such as food, dress, rituals, education curriculum, hospitality to the guests, interaction between the hermits, ascetic and yogic practices, means and resources and the value system of the hermitages. The growth of the chief elements of the hermitages- asceticism,

---

1 Pulsalkar, A.D. and Keith, A.B., (1969), *Bhasa – A Study*, New Delhi,pp.63-84.

2 Altekar, A.S., (1957), *op.cit.*,pp.332-34.

3 See Appendix – II

4 See Appendix –III.

5 See Appendix – IV

Vedic studies, rituals and spiritualism- was studied in chronological order in the literature to throw light on the genesis of the elements and their synthesis. An effort has been made to explain the origin and transformation of these institutions in the light of socio-historical background. A critical approach has also been made to the role played by these hermitages in furthering social change and progress of Indian society.

One of the difficulties one faces in attempting the subject about the Ancient Hermitages is the vastness of literature in which the references to the hermitages are scattered. Secondly, only a small portion of this literature has been translated into English. As such one has to go through an enormous amount of literature to procure the data on the hermitages.

The main works which contain the bulk of information on the hermitages are the *Rāmāyaṇa* and the *Mahābhārata. Mahābhārata* is dated in 28th *Dvāpara Yuga* i.e. between 3076-3138 B.C. and *Rāmāyaṇa* in 24th *Tretā Yuga* which goes back to 1.8 Million years ago as per Indian Astronomical tradition. The chronology of the Vedic literature which contains indirect evidence on hermitages is largely relative. The chronological scheme for the Vedic literature has been adopted here after the standard works of Dr. Ravi Prakash Arya[1].

---

1 Dr. Ravi Prakash Arya, *Bhāratīya kālagaṇanā kā vaijñānika and vaiśvika svarūpa*, Bharatiya Itihasa Samkalan Yojana, Delhi, 1999.

The thesis has been divided into Six Chapters, the details of which are given below:

Chapter one is introductory and it discusses the problem and approach of the thesis.

Chapter two discusses the distribution of hermitages in time and space. The hermitages have been described with special reference to their geographical background, their life style and events connected with them. The description is given in more or less chronological order based on the sequence of the literary works.

The third chapter deals with the life and culture of the hermitages. It describes the daily routine of activities pertaining to their studies, rituals, penances, food collection, treatment of guests and their natural environment.

The fourth chapter deals with the origin and development of the hermitages. It traces the main strands of the culture of hermitages i.e. asceticism, Vedic study and rituals and spiritualism, historically. Besides, it discusses the transformation of the ancient Indian hermitages with the famous universities.

The fifth chapter discusses the role of the hermitages in bringing about social change through the transformation of Indian culture and thought, education, literature and the ethos of the people. It discusses the missionary role played by the hermitages in the dissemination of Indian culture among tribes and peoples and in achieving synthesis of the varied strands and strains.

The sixth chapter contains the conclusions. It summarises the distribution, cultural pattern, genesis and development and the role of the hermitages as revealed by the present research.

****

CHAPTER – II

THE HERMITAGES

The study of the ancient Indian literature, particularly the *Rāmāyaṇa*, the *Mahābhārata*, the Buddhist literature, the *Purāṇas*, and the Classical Sanskrit works of Kālidāsa, Bhavabhūti, Bāṇa etc. throw significant light on the hermitages. These works contain an account of atleast seventy five hermitages.

The earliest reference to the hermitage is found in the *Śatapatha Brāhmaṇa* (3000 B.C.) which mentions the hermitage of Cyvana[1]. But the epics (*Rāmāyaṇa* and *Mahābhārata*) recount the largest number of the hermitages. The *Rāmāyaṇa* records twenty four of the hermitages[2], while the *Mahābhārata* refers to thirty four of them[3]. But it is surprising that only two of the hermitages, namely, the hermitages of Agastya and Vasistha, are common in the lists of the two epics. This can perhaps be explained in terms of time gap and regional differences. The *Rāmāyaṇa* was located in the eastern and the *Mahābhārata* in the western parts of northern India. The *Rāmāyaṇa* is dated by Dr. Ravi Prakash Arya, 1.8 Million years ago. while the *Mahābhārata* has been placed 3128 B.C[4].

---

1 Max Muller, F., (Ed.) *The Sacred Books of the East*, Vol.xii.

2 Shastri, H.P., (1962). *The Rāmāyaṇa of Vālmīki*, Vol. I; London, (1969) Vol.II; (1959) Vol. III.

3 Roy, P.C., *The Mahābhārata of Krishna Dvaipāyana Vyāsa*, (II Ed), Vols. I, II, III, Calcutta.

4 Ravi Prakash Arya (1999)

The Buddhist literature such as *Vinaya Piṭak*[1], *Jātakas*[2] and the accounts of the Buddhist Pilgrims[3] refers to three hermitages, none of which finds mention in the epics.

The *Purāṇas* describe eleven hermitages, five of which have already been included in the *Mahābhārata.* But the hermitages of Aurva, Durvāsā, Gālava, Kapila, Kardam and Sandīpani have been mentioned here for the first time and seem to be a later date than the epics. The Classical Sanskrit literature describes only the earlier hermitages. Kālidāsa (12th Century B.C.) mentions four hermitages. The Agastya's hermitage of these is mentioned in the *Rāmāyaṇa*, the *Mahābhārata*, while the hermitage of Vasiṣṭ ha also occurred in the *Rāmāyaṇa* and the *Mahābhārata* both. But the hermitages of Svarabhaṅga and Sutighna were mentioned earlier only in the *Rāmāyaṇa.* Here it may be explained that Kālidāsa's works are based upon the historical events that have been described either in *Rāmāyaṇa* or *Mahābhārata.*

The later Classical Sanskrit literature records sixteen hermitages. Of these, the hermitage of Agastya has been mentioned in the *Rāmāyaṇa*, The *Mahābhārata* and the works of Kālidāsa, while the hermitages of Dālbhya, Mātaṅga and Vālmīki occurred in the *Rāmāyaṇa* only. The

---

1 Max Muller, F., (Ed.) op.cit., Vols. xiii; xvii; xx.

2 Francis, H.T. and Thomas, E.J. (1916) *Jataka Tales*, Cambridge.

3 Beal (Trs.) (1911), Life of Hiuen Tsiang (by Shaman Hwui Li), London.

hermitages of Kaṇva, Prāśara, Śaunaka and Vyāsa on the other hand are described in the *Mahābhārata*. The hermitage of Vyāsa and Kaṇva occur in the *Mahābhārata* as well as the *Purāṇas*. The hermitage of Cyavana also occurs in the *Mahābhārata*. But the hermitages of Arbunda, Bhairavācārya, Divākara-mitra, Gautama Rahugaṇa, Jābāli, Jahnu, Kukkutarāma and *Vṛṣparvā* are for the first time mentioned only in the Classical Sanskrit literature.

This perhaps indicates a time-lag and a cultural or regional differences in the background of the different literary works. The Buddha's hermitage is not found mentioned in the epics. On the other hand, the *Rāmāyaṇa* generally records the hermitages in the central gangetic valley and the Vindhyas, while the *Mahābhārata* describes the hermitages of the *Madhyadeśa* and the northern hills. The differences in the lists of the above literature, may suggest difference in cultural and geographical background of the authors and the time lag involved. On the other hand certain older hermitages disappeared, while the new ones have emerged. Very few of the hermitages of the epic age continued to survive into the age of the classical Sanskrit literature. Those which survived include the hermitages of Agastya, Dālbhya, Kaṇva, Mātaṅga, Parāśara, Śaunaka, Vālmīki and Vyāsa. A list of the hermitages classified on the basis of their occurrence in the literature of different periods is given in the Appendix II.

The hermitages were generally located in the forests both in the plains and the hills. The proximity of the source of water, generally the rivers and sometimes also the lakes was an important factor that influenced their location.

The distribution of hermitages in the *Rāmāyaṇa* reveals the location of nine of these hermitages on the rivers. Four of these viz. Dālbhya, Bharadvāja, Vālmīki and Anaṅgdeva lay on the Ganges or its tributaries, two of these i.e. Sutighna and Vāman-Viśvāmitra on the Mandākīni and only two of the hermitages i.e. Agastya and Pañcavaṭī are located on the lakes: Śavari on Pampā and Ṛṣiśriṅga on Ṛṣikuṇḍa. Nine of the hermitages are situated in the hilly tract with six of these lying in the Vindhyan ranges. Of these the hermitages of Atri and Vālmīki are located at Citrakuṭa; the Sapatjanas in between Ṛṣyamukha and Kiṣkindhā; Śukra on Śālvala; Niśākara on Vindhya; Agastya on the Vaidūrya Parvat; Trinbindu on the Sumeru mountains and the Vasiṣṭha and Vāmana-Viśvāmitra in the Himalayas. The remaining of the hermitages lie in the plains. Although the *Āśramas* were generally located in the forests, only nine of these have been specifically associated with the forests in the *Rāmāyaṇa.* Daṇḍakāraṇya has seven of these hermitages i.e. those of Vāmandeva, Svarbhaṅga, Mātaṅga, Pañcavaṭī, Agastya, Daṇḍaka and Agastya's brother, while the Janasthāna hermitage is located in the Janasthāna forest, all in the Vindhya region. The hermitage of Gautama lay in a forest near Mithilā.

The *Mahābhārata* mentions eighteen hermitages on different rivers. Of these, the Sarasvati has four, namely, the hermitages of Dadhīchi, Kurukshetra, Vyāsa and of the Kāmyaka forest. Aditi-kuṇḍa and Dvaita-vana were located on the Apagā, while the Suvrata hermitage lay on the Dṛṣ advati. The hermitage of Cyavana was located on the Vadhusara Nadi near Narnaul. The Ganges and its tributaries had five hermitages which included those of Yāja and Upayāja, Vyāsa, Nara-Nārāyaṇa, Bhṛgu and Mārkaṇḍeya. The hermitage of Śaunaka was located on the Gomati, those of Sthūlaśiras and Raivya on the Samonga river or Madhūvilā, while those of Kaṇva on the Mālinī and Bahudā on the Bahudā Nadī.

Only three of the hermitage in the *Mahābhārata* are located on the lakes which, in all probability, represented the depressions in the dry beds of rivers. The hermitage at Atikunda is identified according to tradition with a tank at Amin perhaps on the Apagā near Kurukshetra. The hermitage of Hidimbi lay on Jālivāhana lake, while the Nara, Nārāyaṇa on the Vinda lake.

According to the *Mahābhārata* four of the hermitage lay on the hills. These included the hermitage of Pāṇḍu, Vyāsa, Parāśara and Nara Nārāyaṇa, all located in the Himalayas. Although the hermitages generally lay in the forests, only six of these are clearly associated with forests according to *Mahābhārata.* Two of these lay in the *Kāmyaka* forest, that of Vyāsa in the *Devadāru* forest. The

Śaunaka hermitage was connected with the *Naimiṣa* forest, while the Dhaumya hermitage was located in the Utkochaka forest.

The Buddhist literature mentions only three of the hermitages of which those of Aśoka and Boddhisattva were located in the Himalayas, while the third was located at Ajapālnigrodha. The *Purāṇas* refers to only a single hermitage on the Ganges i.e the hermitage of Kapila. Three of the hermitages according to the *Purāṇas* lay on the hills. Of those the hermitages of Aurva and Durvāsā lay on the Himalayas, while the Gālava on the Chitrakūṭa mountain in the Vindhyan region.

The Classical Sanskrit literature locates two of the hermitage on the rivers, that of the Bhairavācārya near the Sarasvatī, while that of Gautama Rahugaṇa on the Sadānīrā, the modern Gaṇḍaka.

According to this literature only Aurbunda lay on the lake called Abuya, located on Ābu mountain. Besides, the above literature places the hermitage of Vṛṣaparvā on the Himalayas, that of Divākaramitra on the Vindhyas, Aurbunda on the Abu mountain and Jayasena on Yaṣṭivana hill. The Jayasena hermitage was also referred to by Hiuen-Tsang.

The distribution of the hermitages also shows that these were located in the forests in hills or plains along the rivers or on the lakes as in the earlier periods. Only the classical Sanskrit literature, the accounts of Hiuen-Tsang and the *Bhāgvata Purāṇa* locate some of the hermitages in the town or cities.

Hiuen-Tsang refers to a hermitage which has been identified with Lahore[1]. The Classical Sanskrit literature places the hermitage of Bhairavāchārya near the city of Thanesar, that of Jahnu, perhaps at Sultanganj and the Kukkuṭarāma at Patliputra. The *Bhāgavata Puārāṇa* records the hermitage of Sandipani in the town of Avanti (Ujjaini) and that of Kardama at Siddhapura in Gujarat.

A brief account of the hermitages is given below:

1. The hermitages of Agastya

According to the *Rāmāyaṇa* the hermitage of Agastya was located in the Daṅḍaka forest about four miles to the South of the hermitage of his brother[2]. This hermitage has been identified with Agastipuri, Akola, Kolhapura, Shaighaita, Agastya Muni village, Vaidurya Parvata, Vedāraṇya or Agastya Kota mountain[3]. In the *Āraṇyakāṇḍa,* the

---

1 Das, S.K., (1930) *The Educational System of the Ancient Hindus*, Calcutta, p.325.

2 Shastri, H.P. (1969), *op.cit.* Vol.II, II Ed., pp.27-30.

3 Misar Ramgopal, (1951), *Tapo Bhumi* (Hindi), pp.184-88; Bajpai, K.D. et.al. (1967) (Ed.) *The Geographical Encyclopaedia of Ancient and Medieval India*, Part I, Varanasi, P.6; Sharma, J.S. (1978) *The National Geographical Dictionary of India*, New Delhi.

hermitage of Agastya is said to be located on the bank of the Saraju near its confluence with the Ganges[1]. The *Mahābhārata* refers to the visit of Yudhisthira to the hermitage. The *Raghuvañśa* locates it near Pañcavati on the banks of the Godāvarī[2]. Bāṇa, in his Kādambarī, locates it in the Vindhyan forests and points out that the same had since long been deserted[3]. According to Bhavabhūti the hermitage of Agastya was located in the *Daṇḍaka* forest where the sage Agastya dwelt along with many scholars, well versed in the *Sāmaveda*[4]. The hermitage is also said to be visited by Ātareyī to acquire
Upaniṣadika lore[5].

The sage Agastya is known to have given Rāma a gift of bow and arrow and a sword. The above description suggests that the tradition of hermitages was shifting from the Gangetic plains in the *Rāmāyaṇa* to the banks of Godāvarī in *Raghuvañśa.*

2. *Hermitage of Agastya's brother*

While directing Rāma to the hermitage of sage Agastya,

---

1 *Rāmāyaṇa, Āraṇya Kāṇḍa,* 12th Sarga. Eng. Tr. by Dr. Ravi Prakash Arya

2 *Raghuvañśa*, Canto XIII. 34-35.

3 *Kādambarī,* M. Riddings (Eng. Trans.), pp. 18-20.

4 *Uttara-Rāma Carita*, Belvalkar's Eng. Trans, pp.31-33.

5 Quoted by Das, S.K., (1930), *op.cit.*, p.318.

Sutikṣaṇa guided him first to go to the hermitage of Agastya's brother. This was located about four miles to the south of Agastya's hermitage in the fertile plain replete with groves of fig trees[1].

3. *Hermitage of Anangadeva*

Hermitage of Anaṅgadeva was located at the confluence of the Ganges and the Sarayū. The sage lived there along with his pupils. Viśvāmitra visited the place along with Rāma and Lakṣmaṇa[2].

4. Hermitage of Atri

The hermitage was visited by Rāma, Sītā and Lakṣ maṇa in course of their exile according to the *Rāmāyaṇa*[3]. B.C. Law locates it near Citrakūṭa[4]. The hermitage was inhabited by sage Atri and his wife Anusūyā alongwith many other hermits engaged in spiritual penances.

The hermitage is also described in Raghuvamśá by Kālidāsa. Anusūyā was very kind to Sītā and gave her a discourse on the virtues of chastity[5]. She

---

1 Shastri, H.P., (1969), *op.cit.*, Vol. II, pp.22-27.

2 Das, S.K., (1930), *op.cit.*, p. 316.

3 *Rāmāyaṇa, Ayodhyā Kāṇḍa*, 118th *Adhyāya*. Eng. Tr. By Dr. Ravi Prakash Arya.

4 Law, B.C., (1976) *Historical Geography of Ancient India,* Delhi, p.142; Bajpai, K.D. et.al., (1967), *op. cit.*, p. 38; Sharma, J.S., (1972), *op. cit.*

exhorted her to be devoted to her husband and to carry out the conjugal duties as there is none who is a better friend than the husband who protects his wife in all circumstances[1].

5. The hermitage of Bhāradwāja

The hermitage of Bharadwāja was located near the confluence of the Ganges and the Yamunā at Prayāga according to the *Rāmāyaṇa*[2]. The hermitage lay on way from Ayodhyā to Chitrakūta hill. Rāma visited this hermitage while going in exile[3]. On his way back to Ayodhya also he visited the hermitage[4].

The *Mahābhārata* also refers to this place. Drupada, the son of king Prasathanama, a friend of Bhāraduāja, was sent for education to this hermitage. Bhāraduāja was succeeded by his son Droṇa at the hermitage[5].

6. Hermitage of Dālbhya

The hermitage is identified with Dālbhya on the Ganges about 19 miles from Rai Bareli[6]. It was near

---

5 Quoted by Das, S.K., (1930), *op.cit.*, p.323.

1 Shastri, H.P., (1962), *op.cit.*, Vol.i, pp.431-37.

2 *Rāmāyaṇa, Ayodhya Kanda* 54th and 89th Sargas.

3 Law, B.C., (1976), *op.cit.*, p.7; Sharma, J.S., (1978), *op.cit.*, p.35; shastri, H.P., (1962), *op.cit.*, Vol.III, pp.275-96.

4 Shastri, H.P., (1959), *op.cit.*, Vol.III, pp. 305-06.

5 Das, S.K., (1930), *op.cit.* p.317.

6 *JASB*, Vol. IXIX., p.84.

this hermitage that Rāma and Lakṣmaṇa met Sugrīva and his hosts. A fort and the ruins of the two Buddhist stupas are seen at the spot at present[1]. From the description it seems the hermitage was located in the Vindhyan hills.

7. *Hermitages of the Daṇḍaka Forest*

The *Daṇḍaka* Forest was famous for the hermitages of ascetics in the past. According to *Rāmāyaṇa*, the *Daṇḍaka* forest hermitages which were located on a circular hill were visited by Rāma[2]. The site was picturesque one and the huts were thatched with leaves. The sacred fire burnt here surrounded by the articles of worship, *kuśa* grass, guel, water pots, roots and fruits within a groove of trees. Rāma and his party received traditional hospitalities at the hands of the ascetics, observing sacred vows.

8. *Hermitage of Gautama*

According to *Rāmāyaṇa* the hermitage of Gautama was located in a forest near Mithila, the capital town of king Janaka[3]. The spot has been identified with Janakpura or Gonda[4]. Gautama performed

---

1 *Rai Bareli District Gazetteer* by Navil, p.160; Bajpai, K.D. et.al. (Ed.) (1967), *op.cit.*, pp.101-102

2 Shastri, H.P., (1969), *op.cit.*, Vol.II, pp.3-4.

3 *Rāmāyaṇa, Bāla Kāṇḍa*, 48th Sarga, eng. Tr. Dr. Ram Prakash Arya

4 Law, B.C., (1976), *op.cit.*, p.218., Sharma, J.S., (1972), op.cit..

austerities in company with Ahalyā at this hermitage. It was later visited by Vishwāmitra and Rāma on their way to the Svayaṁvara of Sītā. It is said that the hermitage of Gautama was once visited by Indra who seduced Ahalyā, the wife of sage Gautama. The Ṛṣi cursed his wife have known all this. But when she propitiated the Ṛṣi by telling him how Indra impersonated by assuming the form of the sage Gautama, the sage told her that she would be purified by the visit of Rāma to this place[1].

9. *Hermitage of Janasthana Forest*

The *Rāmāyaṇa* in the *Ayodhyā Kāṇda* refers to the hermitages in the *Janasthāna* forest[2]. But the location is not precisely mentioned. The forest was touched by Rāma on his way from Chitrakuta to Panchavati. This suggest the location of the *Janasthāna* forest in between *Chitrakūṭa* and *Pañcavaṭī* in the Vindhyas. Nearby the forest is mentioned the hermitage of Aśva.

Bharata is said to have visited in Rāma in the *Janasthāna* forest on his return from the residence of his maternal uncle. The *Rāmāyaṇa* also refers tob a fact that the sages of *Janasthāna* prepared to leave

---

0.72.

1 Shastri, H.P., (1959), *op.cit.*, Vol.III (Uttar Kāṇḍa), pp.475-76.

2 Shastri, H.P., (1962), *op.cit.*, Vol.I (Ayodhya Kāṇḍa),pp.429-30.

for the Ashva hermitage being oppressed by the *Rakṣasas* because of their enmity to Rāma.

10. *Hermitage of Mātaṅga*

The *Rāmāyaṇa* refers to the hermitage of sage Mātaṅga and locates it in the *Daṇḍakāranya.*[1] This hermitage is also mentioned in the *Kathāsaritsāgara.*[2]

11. *Hermitage of Niśākara*

The *Rāmāyaṇa* mentions the hermitage of sage Niśākara of severe austerities, located at the Vindhyan peak on the shores of the southern sea. Sampāti, the elder brother of Jaṭāyu, is said to have had the vision of the sage Niśākara after regaining consciousness. The correct location of the hermitage has not been worked out.[3]

12. *Hermitage of Pañcvaṭī*

According to *Rāmāyaṇa* Rāma had built his hut near Agastya's hermitage at *Pañcvatī* in the forest while in exile. According to J. S. Sharma it was located on the bank of Godavari.[4] The place was beautified

---

1 *Rāmāyaṇa*, *Araṇya Kāṇḍa*, 73rd Sarga; *Kishkindhya Kāṇḍa*, 11 sarga.

2 *Kathāsaritsāgara*, Penzer (Tr.) V.202; VII.144. 145.149, 151, 152, 156.

3 Shastri, H.P., (1969), *op.cit.*, pp.311-12.

by flowers, trees and springs. Rāma spent the first part of his exile at this hermitage.[1] The spot is also mentioned in the *Mahābhārata.*

13. ***Hermitage of Ṛṣyaśṛṅga***

According to B.C. Law this hermitage was located about 28 miles west of Bhāgalapur and four miles South-west of Bariarpur in Eastern India.[2] The sage Ṛṣyaśṛṅga is said to have meditated at this place according to the *Mahābhārata.* The hermitage is described as situated in a circular valley formed by the Maira hill (Maruk hill) which contained a ṛṣ ikuṇḍa that received the combined waters of a hot and a cold springs. The *Mahābhārata* also refers to a hermitage of sage Kaśyapa, the father of sage Ṛṣyaśṛṅga, located on the bank of the Kauśikī nadī near the hermitage of Viśvāmitra.[3] The Aśrama is also mentioned by the Kathāsaritasāgara.[4] But according to Hari Parsad Shastri the proximity of the Ṛṣikuṇḍa to the Ganges, the scene where a public women was sent by Lomapāda, the King of Aṅga to entice the young sage, suggests the Ṛṣ

---

4 Sharma, J.S., (1972), *op.cit.*, p.140; Bajpai, K.D. et.al. (1967), *op.cit.,* p.6.

1 Shastri, H.P., (1969), *op.cit.*, pp.34-35.

2 Law, B.C., (1976), op.cit., p.256; quoted by Sharma J.S. (1972), *op.cit.,* p.160.

3 *Mahābhārata*, 109th and 110th adhyāyas.

4 Quoted by Das, S.K. (1930), *op.cit.*, pp.320-21.

ikuṇḍa to be the spot where the sage Ṛṣyaśṛnga and his father performed austerities in the Rāmāyaṇa.[1]

14. ***Hermitage of Śavarī***

The hermitage of Śavarī is said to be located in South India according to B.C. Law.[2] Formerly, the hermitage of sage Mātaṅga and his disciples was located here. The hermitage lay on the western bank of the Pampā lake shaded on all sides by trees. The lake abounded in lotuses and in its surroundings grew wild fruits in abundance.

Rāma visited the hermitage of Śavarī who greeted him with the traditional mode. Śavarī who had grown extremely old wore matted locks of hair, meager garments and skin of black deer.[3]

15. ***The hermitage of Saptajanas***

The *Saptajana* hermitage is described as located between

Ṛṣyamukha and the Kiskindhā mountains according to the *Rāmāyaṇa.*[4] This vast hermitage abounded in pleasant gardens and groves, fruits, roots and water and was called *Saptajanas.* The seven munis are said to have undertaken rigid vows by lying in the

---

1 Shastri, H.P., (1962), op. cit., Vol.I, pp.27-28.
2 Law, B.C., (1976), op.cit., p.18.
3 Shastri, H.P., (1962), op.cit., Vol.I., pp.156-158.
4 Shastri, H.P., (1969), op.cit., Vol.II., pp.198-200.

water at this hermitage. Rāma is known to have visited the hermitage and paid homage to the sages.[1] It is possible that the hermitage was so called because of the association of the region with seven tribes in ancient times.

16. Hermitage of Śukrācārya

The location of the hermitage of Śukrācārya is not mentioned precisely in the *Rāmāyaṇa* which recounts a story connected with this hermitage.[2]

According to the legend a king Daṇḍa by name, ruled at Madhumanta. One day the king happened to visit the hermitage of Śukrācārya. He saw the eldest daughter of the sage in the forest land. The king seduced Aruja forcefully despite her protests and returned to his town. When the sage learnt about it, he cursed the king that he will perish in seven nights along with his children, infantry and cavalry. He asked his daughter to stay in the hermitage till her deliverance and himself found a dwelling elsewhere.

17. *The Hermitage of Sutighna*

The hermitage is described in the *Rāmāyaṇa* and the *Raghuvañśa.*[3] Rāma was directed by Śarabhaṅga to

---

1 Ibid.

2 Shastri, H.P., (19159), Vol.III., pp.591-93.

follow the course of the mandākīni river to reach Sutīkṣṇa's hermitage. Having crossed several deep rivers Rāma saw a high mountain on which was located the Sutighna hermitage in a solitary spot. It was singled out by the garlands and barks spread there. Sutīkṣṇa welcomed Rāma and requested him to stay at the hermitage where roots and fruits were available in all seasons.[1]

18. ***Hermitage of Śukra***

The hermitage of Śukra is stated to be located in the Kingdom of Daṇḍa in between the Vindhya and Śaivāla mountains according to the *Rāmāyaṇa.*[2] He was accompanied by many pupils including the king Daṇḍa.[3]

19. ***Hermitage of Svarabhaṅga***

The *Rāmāyaṇa* describes the hermitage of Svarabhaṅga in the *Daṇḍakāraṇya* among many other hermitages.[4] All these hermitages resounded by the recitation of the Vedas. This hermitage is also mentioned in the *Raghuvaṅśa.*[5]

---

3 Quoted by Das, S.K., (1930), *op.cit.*, p.318.

1 Shastri, H.P., (1969), op.cit., Vol.II, pp.15-17.

2 *Rāmāyaṇa, Uttara Kāṇḍa*; 79th *Sarga.*

3 *Rāmāyaṇa*, *Uttarakaṇḍa*, 80th *Sarga*; Das, S.K., (1930), *op.cit.*, p.317.

4 Shastri, H.P., (1969), *op.cit.*, Vol.II, pp.10-15; *Rāmāyaṇa, Araṇyakaṇḍa*, 1st, 8th and 11th Sargas.

5 Das, S.K., (1930), *op.cit.*, p.318.

20. *Hermitage of Rajarṣi Triṇabindu*

The *Rāmāyaṇa* locates the hermitage of Rajarṣi Triṇabindu by the side of the Sumeru mountain.[1] The sage Pulastya son of the Prajāpati, is said to have undertaken ascetic practices and recitation of the *Veda* there. Once, being distracted he cursed young maidens that one who fell under his gaze would instantly conceive. The daughter of the sage Triṇabindu who had not heard about the curse approached the hermitage of Pulastya and became pregnant. On knowing the whole story the sage Trinabindu along with his daughter approached Pulastya and requested him to accept her as his wife. Sage Pulastya agreed to marry her.[2] He blessed her of a son like himself.[3]

21. *The Hermitage of Vālmīki*

The hermitage of Vālmīki[4] has been placed in North India by J. S. Sharma.[5] It has been described in the *Rāmāyaṇa* as located at the *Citrakūṭa* hill on the Tamasā river.[6]

---

1 Ibid.

2 Law, B.C., (1976), *op.cit.*, p.136; Sharma, J.S., (1972), *op.cit.*,p.181.

3 Shastri, H.P., (1959), *op.cit.*,Vol.III, *Rāmāyaṇa, Uttara Kāṇḍa*, pp.377-79.

4 Shastri, H.P., (1962), *op.cit.*, Vol.I pp.301-303; Shastri, H.P., (1959) *op.cit.*,Vol.III, pp.530-32, 568, 69, 610-22.

5 Sharma, J.S., (1972) *op.cit.*, p.187.

6 *Rāmāyaṇa* (*Ayodhya Kanda*, 56th Sarga; Uttar Kāṇḍa, 45th Sarga).

But according to Bhavabhūti, the hermitage was situated on the Ganges.[1] In the *Kathāsaritsāgara* the hermitage is mentioned not far from the spot called *Pañcvaṭī.* It seems the tradition shifted in different ages. Rāma and his party were entertained here when Śatrunghna stopped here for one night while on an expedition against Lavaṇa. Vālmīki explained to him that this hermitage was originally connected with king Sudāsa of the family of Raghu.[2]

Kalidasa refers to the hermitage of Vālmīki in his *Raghuvaṅśa*.[3] Vālmīki is said to have taught *Vedas*, *Vedāṅgas* and the art of singing to the twin sons of Rāma and Ātreyī in the hermitage. According to the *Rāmāyaṇa,* there resided many pupils in this hermitage including Bhāradvāja, a well known scholar in the lore of *Śāstras.*[4] It was at this hermitage that Sītā is known to have given birth to her twin sons – Lava and Kuśa.

22. *Hermitage of Vāmana and Viśvāmitra*

B.C. Law locates the hermitage of Vāmana and Viśvāmitra at Buxar in the Shahabad district of Bihar.[5] According to the *Rāmāyaṇa*, the female

---

1 *Belvalkar* (Tr.) *Uttara-Rāma-Carita*, Acts IV and V, pp.31-33.

2 *Rāmāyaṇa, Uttarakāṇda*, 65th Sarga.

3 *Raghuvaṅśam*, Canto XIV. 38, XV.74.

4 *Rāmāyaṇa, Bālakāṇḍa* 2nd Sarga.

5 Law, B.C., (1976) *op.cit.*, p.6.

demon Tāḍakā was killed by Rāma at this spot.[1] But it locates the hermitage in the Himalayas between Kanchanjangha and Dhavalagiri on the bank of the river Mandākīnī.[2]

Viṣṇu is known to have taken an incarnation of Vāmana and attained perfection in austerity at this holy spot. It was here that the twin princes of Ayodhyā received training in the art of warfare under the able guidance of Viśvāmitra.[3]

23. ***Hermitage of Vāmanadeva***

The *Rāmāyaṇa* locates the hermitage of *Vāmanadeva* in the *Daṇḍakāraṇya* which was later on occupied by Viśvāmitra.[4]

24. ***Hermitage of Vasiṣṭha***

The hermitage, according to B.C. law, was situated in the Aravali range at Mount Abu.[5] But Kalidasa locates it in the Himalayas in the Raghuvañśa.[6] The hermitage was once visited by Viśvāmitra also. The *Rāmāyaṇa* gives a graphic description of it.[7] The

---

1 Misar Ramgopal (1951), *op.cit.*, pp.211-12; *Rāmāyaṇa, Bālakāṇḍa*, Ch.26.

2 *Rāmāyaṇa, Kiṣkindhā Kāṇḍa*, Ch.43.

3 Shastri, H.P., (1962), *op.cit.*, Vol.I, pp.66-67.

4 Das. S.K., 1930*), op.cit.,* pp.318-19.

5 Law, B.C., (1976), *op.cit.,* p.335.

6 Das, S.K., (1930), *op.cit.*, p.317.

7 *Rāmāyaṇa, Bālakānda*, 51st Sarga; 52 Sarga.

Rāmāyaṇa also mentions about the hermitage being visited by King Daśratha.[1] The *Mahābhārata* also mentions the hermitage.[2] The *Raghuvañśa* states that Dalīpa and his queen desirous of having a son once visited the hermitage.[3] The *Rāmāyaṇa* describes the hermitage as a beautiful spot and adorned with various kinds of flowers, creepers and trees[4] . It was here that Vasiṣṭha is known to have imparted instruction to his disciples in the spiritual knowledge. He taught them the Vedas and the Dharmaśāstras[5].

Since the hermitage is said to have been visited by Daśaratha and Dalipa, its location cannot be far away from Ayodhyā. Hence the possibility of the Vasiṣṭha's hermitage being located either in the Gangetic plains or in the Himalayas to the north seems to be more plausible.

25. *Hermitage at Aditikuṇḍa*

The tank at Amin, five miles to the south of Kurushetra, has been identified with the *Aditikuṇḍa* of literature[6]. Once there existed the hermitage of

---

1 *Rāmāyaṇa, Uttara Kāṇda.*

2 *Mahābhārata Vanaparva*, 101st Adhyaya.

3 Das, S.K., (1930), *op.cit.*, p.317.

4 Shastri, H.P., (1962), *op.cit.*, pp.106-08.

5 Sen, R.R., (1909), *The Triumph of Valmīki*, Chittong, pp.7010.

6 Bajpai, K.D. et.al., (1967), *op.cit.*, p.5.

sage Kaśyapa and his consort Aditi[1]. Near the pond is situated a Śiva temple at present.

26. **Hermitage at Bahudā**.

The river is named Bahudā because the severed arm of sage Likhita is said to have been restored after he had bathed in it[2]. The *Śiva Purāṇa*, however, records the transformation of Gauri, the grandmother of Māndhātā, into the river Bahudā by the curse of her husband Prasenjit[3]. The hermitage of Saṅkha and Likhita are said to have been situated on the banks of this river according to *Mahābhārata*[4]. But no precise location about the river and the hermitage is given.

27. ***Hermitage of Bāka***

The *Mahābhārata* refers to the hermitage of Bāka[5] which resounded with Vedic hymns. But the works give no precise location about the hermitage.

28. ***Hermitage of Bhārgava***

The location of the hermitage of Bhārgava is not given in the *Mahābhārata*. But the work records that

---

1 *Mahābhārata*, 83-184; *Padma Purāṇa*, 1.27-70.

2 Bajpai, K.D., et.al. (1967), *op.cit.*, p.46; *Mahābhārata*, XII Ch.22; Hv. Ch.12.

3 *Śiva Purāṇa*, Pt. VI Ch.60.

4 *Mahābhārata*, XII. 23. 18-19.

5 *Mahābhārata*, *Śalyaparva*, 42nd Adhyāya.

Bhārgava had destroyed the world 21 times. He is known to have had great mastery over all the weapons.

Droṇa, whose wife Kṛpi gave birth to Aśvatthāmā, had a great ambition to become a great archer of the time. He approached Bhārgava with a request to teach him the art of archery. Bhārgava accepted Droṇa as his pupil and made him master of all weapons[1].

Radheya (Karṇa) is also stated to be very keen to learn archery. He also approached Bhārgava who taught him all the weapons including the *Brahmāstra* and the powerful *Bhārgavāstra.* But when Bhārgava learnt that Radheya was not a Brahmin, he cursed him that his memory will fail him when he would be desperately in need of an *astra.* But he was blessed to be known as a great archer on the earth[2].

29. *Hermitage of Bhṛgu*

The *Mahābhārata* locates the Bhṛgu *Tīrtha* at the confluence of the Ganges and the Sarayū. According to the *Mahābhārata*, Paraśurāma regained his energy at this spot, after he had been deprieved of it by Rāma earlier[3]. It was at this hermitage that the king Vītahavya took shelter and became a *Brāhmaṇa*[4].

---

1 Subrāmaniam, Kamala, (1965), *Mahābhārata*, *Bombay*, p.40.

2 Subrāmanim, Kamala (1965), *op. cit.*, pp.47-50.

30. *Hermitage of Cyavana*

The *Mahābhārata* mentions the hermitage of Cyavana Ṛṣi on the bank of the river Vadhusara. This river has been identified with the modern Duhan stream near Narnaul in Haryana, according to a local tradition[1]. The *Śatapatha Brāhmaṇa* mentions that the sage Cyavana became younger by bathing here and married the daughter of king Śaryāti named Sukanyā[2]. The *Mahābhārata* also recounts a story of the marriage of Cyavana with Sukanyā. Cyavana was the son of the great sage Bhṛgu. He begin to practice austerities by the side of lake by adopting the *vīra* pose. In the course of time his body was covered by an ant-hill. Once king Śaryāti, the ruler of the region, happened to visit the lake along with his beautiful daughter Sukanyā. On seeing the young girl the sage become torn with lust. The girl out of curiosity pierced the eyes of the *ṛṣi* covered with ant-hill with thorns. Being agitated the *Ṛṣi* cursed the forces of the king. When the king approached the sage for forgiving the fault of her daughter, Cyavana asked for the hand of the beautiful girl as his bride as a condition for

---

3 *Mahābhārata*, III.99.86.50.

4 Law, B.C., (1976), op.cit., p.72; Sharma, J.S. (1972), *op.cit.*, 39; Brajpai, K.D. et.al. (Ed.) (1967); *op.cit.*, P.70

1 Bhargava, P.L., (1971), *India in the Vedic Age*, Lucknow, pp.132-133.

2 Bajpai, K.D. et. al. (1967), *op.cit.*, p.98.

forgiving them. The king agreed and gave his daughter in marriage to the sage to attend him, his guests and the sacred fire[1].

31. ***Hermitage of Dadhīcha***

The hermitage of Dadhīcha was located in the Kurukshetra region on the bank of the Sarasvati *Nadī*[2]. A story goes in the *Mahābhārata* that in the *Kṛta* age there lived certain tribes of *Dānavas* who pursued the *Devas*. The *Dānavas* fought under the leadership of *Vṛtra*, while the *Devas* were headed by Indra. The gods having resolved to destroy *Vṛtra* approached Brahmā. The latter asked them to go to Dadhicī Ṛṣi, who would renounce his body to make his bones available for making the powerful weapon of *Vajra* with the help of which they would be able to destroy the demons. The *Devas* approached Dadhīca and did as directed. Dadhīca gave up his life for the services of the *Devas*[3] which ultimately led to the success of the *Devas*.

32. ***Hermitage of Devasama***

The *Mahābhārata* refers to the hermitage of Devasama, the pupil of Agastya as located on a mountain[4]. But no precise description is given about

---

1 Roy, P.C., *op.cit.,* Vol.III, II Ed., pp.265-66.

2 Bajpai, K.D. et.al. (1967), *op.cit.,* p.98

3 Roy, P.C. *op.cit.,* Vol.II, pp. 225-26.

the mountain or the hermitage. Devasama had a favourite pupil in Bipula[1].

33. ***Hermitage of Dhaumya***

The *Mahābhārata* mentions the hermitage of Dhaumya at Utkochaka[2]. But the precise location of it is not known. The epic mentions that Arjuna asked a Gandharva to tell about a Brāhmaṇa knowing Veda and suitable for being appointed as their priest when in exile.

The *Gandharva* pointed out to the hermitage of Dhaumya at Utkochaka. He was the younger brother of Devala. The Pāṇḍavas then approached Dhaumya who agreed to function as the priest of the Pāṇḍavas. Having received the benedictions by the priest, the Pāṇḍavas resolved to go to the *Swayaṁvara* of the princess of the Pañcāla kingdom.

34. ***Hermitage of Droṇa***

Droṇa, according to the *Mahābhārata*, came to stay with the preceptor of the princes. Bhiṣma introduced his grandsons, the children of Kuru and Pāṇḍu to Droṇa and made many valuable presents to the

---

4 Bajpai, K.D., et.al., (Ed.) (1967) *op.cit.*, p.108.

1 Das, S.K., (1930), *op.cit.*, p.320.

2 Roy, P.C., *op.cit.*, Vol.I., pp.417-18.

preceptor. Droṇa accepted the pupils gladly. The story goes that Droṇa told the pupils to promise to accomplish a particular purpose when they are skilled in arms.

The Kuru princes kept silent. But Arjuna vowed to accomplish it. He became the most favourite of the guru by his devotion to the service of Droṇa and also to the arms. Arjuna was taught the art of fighting on horse-back, on the back of elephant, on car and on ground. He also learnt fighting with mace, sword, lance, spear and the dart. He learnt the use of many weapons and fighting with men at the same time. Ekalavya, the son of Hiraṇyadhanus, king of the Niṣādas, approached Droṇa for learning the art of warfare. But Droṇa did not accept him as his pupil in archery, as he happened to be a *Niṣāda* (a non-royality pupil) and might excel in course of time his pupils from royalty. Ekalavya, however, touched the feet of the *Guru* and went to the forest. He began to practise the use of the weapons having placed the clay image of Droṇa before him and thus acquired great skill and fame.

Two of Droṇa's pupils, Duryodhana and Bhīma, became accomplished in the use of mace, Aśvatthāmā excelled everyone in the science of arms, Nakula and Sahadeva surpassed all others in the handling of sword and Yudhisthira became an excellent car-warrior. But Arjuna excelled every one in respect of intelligence, resourcefulness, strength and preserverance[1].

35. *Hermitage of Pāṇḍavas at Dvaitavana*

The Pāṇḍavas are mentioned in the *Mahābhārata* to have stayed in the *Dvaitavana* after passing through the *Kāmyaka Vana* on the Saraswati. The location of the *Dvaitavana* as well as the hermitage of the Pāṇḍavas is not precisely given. Traditionally, the *Dvaitavana* is associated with the region where the modern village of *Debana* (near Kaithal) is situated. The forest was more like a wild garden with tall trees. Markaṇḍeya is mentioned to have visited the Pāṇḍavas in their hermtage and prophesied that Yudhiṭhira who walked the forest like Rāma would rule the world after his trial was over. Yudhiṣṭhira enjoyed the company of *Ṛṣis* in this forest and came to realize the true values of the things[2].

36. *Hermitage of Gautama Sāradvat*

The *Mahābhārata* mentions the hermitage of sage Gautama who had a son named Sāradvat. The son

---

1 Roy, P.C., *op.cit.*, Vol.I, pp.312-16.

2 Subrāmaniam, Kamala 1965), *op.cit.*, pp.190-192, Roy, P.C., *op.cit.*, Vol.II, II Ed., pp-53-57.

was so named because he was told to be born a expert of archery and to have great aptitude for the study of the science of the weapons. Once a celestial damsel named Janapadī visited the hermitage of Gautama. The incident resulted in the birth of twin-children who were deserted. The children were later picked up by a soldier of king Śantanu while the monarch was out for hunting in the forest. He handed over the infants to the king who brought them up and named them Kṛpa and Kṛipī. Sāradvat later on learnt about the where abouts of his children and brought them to his hermitage. He taught them the four branches of knowledge. Soon Kṛpa became eminent in the science of arms. The Kurus, the Pāṇḍavas, the Yādavas, the Vṛṣṇis and many other princes received their training at his hands[1].

37 ***Hermitage of Hiḍimbi***

The hermitage of Hiḍimbi has been mentioned in the *Mahābhārata,* but no precise location is given. It is stated in the epic that when Pāṇḍavas reached at the hermitage of Hiḍimbi they were taken by her to *Jalivāhan* lake, she constructed a beautiful hermitage for them and gave them good food. It was here that Bhīma is said to have married Hiḍimbi and lived happily with her visiting many rivers, mountains and hermitages for seven months. The Pāṇḍavas

1 Roy, P.C., *op.cit.*, Vol.II, pp.303-304

were visited by Vyāsa at this spot. He told Kunti that Hiḍimbi will bear a son to Bhīma who will be famous for his valour and fearlessness all over the world. But he advised them to move to the city of *Ekachakrā* after the birth of Ghaṭotkacha. The story goes that they did as advised by Vyāsa and Hiḍimbi and her son stayed back at the hermitage[1].

38. *Hermitage of Jamadagni*

The location of the hermitage is not precisely given in the *Mahābhārata*[2]. The story relates that Jamadagni, who had obtained mastery over the entire Veda and had become famous for his austerities, paid a visit to king Prasenajit and demanded the hand of his daughter Reṇukā in marriage. After the marriage Jamadagni along with his wife came to reside in a hermitage and began to perform penences. Jamadagni got five sons. Parśurāma, who was the youngest, was superior to all in merit. Once Reṇukā happened to be infatuated by the king Chitraratha. When she reached the hermitage Jamadagni perceived the misdeed of his wife and asked Parśurāma to kill his wicked mother. Parśurāma killed her with an axe and earned the appreciation of his father. In another instance the son of Kṛtavīrya, the king of the region near the sea

---

1 Subrāmaniam, Kamala (1965), op.cit., pp.78-79.

2 Roy, P.C., op.cit., Vol.III, (ii Ed.) pp.254-55).

shore, happened to visit the hermitage. The wife of Jamadagni received him hospitably. But the warrior was not pleased with the reception accorded to him. He by force carried her off the hermitage. When Parśurāma came home his father narrated the whole story. Parśurāma pursued Kṛtavīrya's son and killed him. On this the kinsmen of the prince became excited and killed Jamadagni while Parśurāma was away.

39. *Hermitage at Kāmyaka*

The *Mahābhārata* refers to the visit of Pāṇḍavas to the *Kāmyaka* forest which was the favourite haunt of the sages[1]. The Kāmyaka forest was situated on the banks of the Saraswati and formed a level plain. The Pāṇḍavas desirous of living in that forest went from the banks of the Ganges to Kurukshetra. They performed ablution in the holy water of Saraswati, Dṛṣadvati and the Yamunā and went from one forest to another in a westerly direction. At last they came to the *Kāmyaka Vana.* They were visited by Vidura when they were living in a hermitage in the Kāmyaka forest.

Mārkeṇdeya and Krishna also visited them there. It was here that Yudhiṣṭhira requested Mārkaṇḍeya to tell the greatness of the *Brāhmaṇas.* Mārkaṇḍeya

---

1 Roy, P.C., *op.cit.*, Vol.II, pp.15-17.

narrates a story and tells that death has no power over the *Brāhmaṇas.* They performed their sacred duties and fear no death. They speak well of the *Brāhmaṇas.* They entertain their guests and their dependents before they partake. They are peaceful, austere, charitable and forebearing. They live in sacred places of great spiritual power[1].

40. *The Hermitage of Kaṇva*

The hermitage of sage Kaṇva was located on the bank of river Mālini in Sāharanpur district. But according to the *Mahābhārata* it is mentioned as situated on river Chambal, while the *Padmapurāṇa* mentions it on the river Narmada[2]. The *Kathāsaritsāgara* mentions a king named Chandrāvaloka who visited this hermitage in course of his hunting expedition. He was advised by Kaṇva to give up the cruel act of death. On King's promise to renounce hunting the sage Kaṇva gave his daughter in marriage to him. It also records the story of Vyāghrasena, a minister of king Mṛgasikhādatta, who visited this hermitage to receive the advice of the sage[3].

---

1 Roy, P.C., *op.cit.*, Vol.III, (II Ed.) pp. 383.90.
2 Law, B.C., (1976), *op.cit.*, p.89; Sharma, J.S., (1972), op.cit.,p.96.
3 Das, S.K., (1930), *op.cit.*, p.321.

There lived many sages skilled in the art of constructing platforms of yajña and in the rules of rituals. They were well conversant with logic, the knowledge of the *Vedas* and *Vedāṅgas*, astrology, properties of matter and zoology etc.[1]

41. ***Women's Hermitage at Kurukshetra***

The *Mahābhārata* mentions an important hermitage in the Kāmyaka forest near Kurukshetra. Here lived two women ascetics leading a life of *Brahmacharya*. One of these women was *Brāhmaṇa*, while the other was the daughter of King Śāṇḍilya. Both of them attained spiritual pre-eminence.[2]

The *Mahābhārata* refers to Madhuka, Mango, Plaksa and Nyagrodha trees growing in the hermitage.[3]

42. ***Hermitage of Mārkaṇdeya***

The *Mahābhārata* places the hermitage at the confluence of Gomati and the Ganges.[4] But the *Padma Purāṇa* refers to sage Mārkaṇḍeya practising asceticism at the confluence of the Sarayū and the

---

1 Roy, P.C., *op. cit.*, Vol.I, pp. 167-168

2 Das, S.K., (1930), *op.cit.*, pp.322; Mookerjee, R.K., (1947), *Ancient Indian Education,* London, p.335.

3 Yadav, K.C., (1968), *Haryana Studies in History and Culture,* Kurukshetra, pp.13-14.

4 Sharma, J.S., (1972), op.cit., p.120; Law, B.C., (1976), op.cit., p.111.

Ganges. The hermitage was visited by Bhiṣma according to the *Mahābhārata.*[1]

43. *Hermitage of Nara and Nārāyaṇa*

The *Mahābhārata* locates the hermitage of Nara and Nārāyaṇa at mountain Kailash.[2] There lived a host of sages subsisting on fruits and roots having their senses under control and leading the *Vānaprastha* mode of life. The Pāṇḍavas visited the hermitage of Nara and Nārāyaṇa and offered oblations to the *Pitras,* the gods and the *Ṛṣis* in the sacred waters of the Bhāgirathī. They saw the holy lake Vinda and the mountain Maināka. They resided there with the Brāhmaṇas, offering oblations and practising meditation for some time[3].

44. *Hermitage of Pāṇḍu*

According to the *Mahābhārata,* the hermitage of Pāṇḍu was located on the southern slopes of the snowy Himalayas. Pāṇḍu lived at this hermitage with his queens Kuntī and Mādrī after the compaign. During his stay in the forest he killed a ṛṣ i who cursed him. Consequently, he decided to stay in the forest for rest of his life to attain peace. His wife Kuntī gave birth to Yudhiṣhṭhira, Bhīm and Arjuna, while Mādrī bore Nakula and Sahadeva.

---

1 *Mahābhārata*, Vanaparva, Ch.84.

2 Roy P.C., op.cit., Vol.III, (II Ed.) pp.308-09.

3 Ibid.

The *Nāmakaraṇa sanskāra* of the children was performed by the Ṛṣis living in the valley of Śatasṛṅga. Later the young princes received their early education from them. The *Upanayana* ceremony of the children was performed by Kaśyapa, a priest of Vasudeva, the brother of Kuntī. The young princes were trained in the use of arms by Śuka, the son of Śaryati, who lived in the forest and was an unrivalled archer. Being pleased with the performance of Arjuna his preceptor gave him a holy bow as a mark of his appreciation[1].

45. ***Hermitage of Parāśara.***

The *Mahābhārata* mentions this hermitage but gives no precise location for it.[2] The *Parāśara Saṁhitā*[3] however, locates it at Badarikā[4] Bana[5] and Somadeva[6] also refers to the hermitage of Badarikā. Perhaps Badarika was the same as Adbadri (Ādi Badri) a *tirtha* in the Śivaliks in Ambala District.

The story goes in the *Mahābhārata* that the sage Vaśiṣtha had a son Saktri by name. He was killed by a Rākṣasa in a different forest. The latter's wife Adṛsyanti gave birth to a son called Parāsara. Sage

---

1 Subrāmaniam, Kamala, (1965), *op.cit.*, pp. 25-29.

2 Das, S.K., (1930), *op.cit.*, p.320.

3 *Prāśara Saṁhitā*, Ch. 1, Sl. 6-7.

4 Roy, P.C., (1969), *op.cit.*, Vol.I, (II Ed.), pp.410-415.

5 Riddings, C.M. (Trs.) *Kādambrī*, p.216.

6 Penzer (Tr.) *Kathāsaritsāgar*, Vol.I, pp.58,59,79; Vol.II, p.36

Vaśisṭha performed usual Sanskāras of his grandson. On one occasion the child addressed Vaśisṭha as father in the presence of his mother. Adṛsyanti told him that his father had been devouvered by a Rākṣ asa and the sage was his grandfather. The child was very sorry and resolved to destroy all the Rākṣasa. In course of time Parāśara performed a grand Rākṣ asa sacrifice and began to consume the Rākṣasas indiscriminately. On seeing this, the sage Atri approached him to stop the sacrifice, Pulastya also came there. They told Parāśara that in his sacrifice he was slaughtering even the innocent Rākṣasas who knew nothing of his father's death. It behoves a Brāhmaṇa devoted to asceticism not to destroy any creature. Peace is the highest virtue. We should establish it and we should no more be an instrument in destroying the innocent. This advise brought the sacrifice to an and.[1]

46. ***Hermitage of Raivya***

The hermitage of Raivya was located on the river Samaṅga according to the *Mahābhārata*[2]. It was here that the sages Bharadvāja and Raivya, who were friends, dwelt. Raivya is said to have had two sons Arvavaśu and Paravaśu, while Bharadvāja had Yavakri the only son. Raivya and his sons were well

---

1 Roy, P.C., *op.cit.,* Vol.I, (II Ed.), pp.410-15.

2 Roy P.C., *op.cit.*, Vol.III, (II Ed.), pp.290-94.

versed in the *Vedas*. But Bharadvāja was known for asceticism. Yavakri felt slighted by the *Brāhmaṇas* who gave great respect to Raivya and his sons for the knowledge of the *Vedas*, Yavakri performed severe austerities by exposing his body to the flaming fires. Indra advised Yavakri to learn the *Vedas* from the lips of a preceptor rather than destroying himself like that. He granted him boons that the *Vedas* will become manifest to him and to his father.

Bharadvāja told his son to be vigilant and not to approach Raivya who was of an irritable temper. But when Yavakri went to the hermitage of Raivya and fell in love with the daughter-in-law of Raivya. The sage Raivya became very angry and killed Yavakri.

47. ***Hermitage of Saradbāna***

The hermitage has been described in the *Mahābhārata* as a beautiful spot.[1] It was inhabited by a great Ṛṣi Saradbāna who was well versed in Vedic lores. The location of the hermitage is not precisely given.

48. ***Hermitage of Śamika***

---

1 *Mahābhārata*, *Ādiprava*, 130th adhyāya.

The *Mahābhārata* described the hermitage of Śamika Ṛṣi who performed asceticism and was well versed in the Vedas.[1] The Ṛṣi had a well known pupil Gauramukha by name. The location of the hermitage is not known.

49. *Hermitage of Śaunaka*

The *Mahābhārata* refers to the hermitage of Śaunaka as located in the *Naimiṣa* forest on the bank of the Gomati. The hermitage was presided by Śaunaka, who was its *Kulapati.* The place is also mentioned in the *Pañcaviṁsa Brāhmaṇa*, *Padma Purāṇa*, the *Agnipurāṇa*, and the *Yoginitantra.*[2] It was here that the *Purāṇas* were compiled.

Śaunaka performed a twelve year's sacrifice at this hermitage and a vast number of learned scholars were invited to it. The sacrifice was accompanied by discourses of learned men on religious, philosophical and scientific topics[3].

The scholars included the specialists in each of the four *Vedas*, the six *Vedāṅgas*, *Śikṣā* (Phonetics), *Chhanda* (metrics), *Vyākaraṇa* (grammer), *Jyotiśa* (astronomy), *Kalpasūtras* (science of allegorical rituals) and *Nirukta*, (science of etymology),

---

1 *Mahābhārata*, *Ādiprava*, 41st adhyāya.
2 Sharma, J.S., (1972), *op.cit.*, pp.127-28.
3 Das, S.K., (1930), *op.cit.*, P.232

logicians knowing the principles of *Nyāya*, *Vedānta* and those well versed in *Dharma*. There were also specialists in the physical sciences, the architecture of *yajña* altars, and zoologists having knowledge of monkeys and birds.[1]

50. ***Hermitage of Śrutaśravā***

The location of the hermitage is not precisely mentioned in the *Mahābhārata*. It is stated that king Janamejaya, the son of Parikṣit, noticed the hermitage of Śrutaśravā who was deeply engaged in ascetic devotions. Janamejaya requested Śrutaśravā to permit his son Somasravā to be appointed his *Purohita*. Śrutaśravā permitted it. But he made it clear that his son had a habit of granting to the *Brāhmaṇas* anything they begged off. Janamejaya accepted the condition and told his brothers about the appointment of the *Purohita*. He asked them to comply with any instruction from the *Purohita* without examination. The king after issuing instructions to his brothers marched against the territory of Takṣaśilā and brought the same under his sway.[2]

51. ***Hermitage of Sthulaśiras***

---

1 Roy, P.C., *op.cit.,* Vol.I, pp.1017; 'Purāṇa; All India Kashiraj Trust, Varanasi, 1968, Vol.xi, No.I, pp.27-34.

2 Roy, P.C., *op.cit.,* pp.36-37.

The *Mahābhārata* mentions the hermitage of Sthulaśiras as located at Kardamilā on river Samaṅga or Madhuvilā.[1] In this hermitage the sage lived a life devoid of anger and ego. He was well versed in the *Vedas* and practised asceticism.

52. ***The Hermitage of Suvrata***

The *Mahābhārata* mentions the hermitage of Suvrata located in the plains of the *Dṛṣadvatī* river.[2] But there is no more precise description about its location.

53. ***Hermitage of Śvetaketu***

The *Mahābhārata* records the hermitage of Śvetaketu[3]. But its location is not given precisely. The hermitage was graced by the coconut trees. Śvetaketu, the son of Uddālaka, received the gift of speech from the goddess Sarasvatī and went to the yajña of king Janaka along with his nephew Aṣṭ āvakra. Though a child, he defeated his opponents in a literary contest at Janaka's yajña.

54. ***Hermitage of Uddālaka***

The location of the hermitage of Uddālaka is not given precisely in the *Mahābhārata*.[4] Uddālaka was a great sage and had among his pupils one Kahora

---

1 Roy, P.C., *op.cit.*, Vol.III (II Ed.), p. 290.

2 *Mahābhārata, Vanaparva*, 90th adhyāya.

3 Roy, P.C., op.cit., Vol.III (II Ed.).

4 *Mahābhārata, Vanaparva*, 131st adhyāya.

who served the preceptor very faithfully. Uddālaka gave him the hand of his daughter in marriage as reward for it.

55. *Hermitage of Vyāsa*

The *Mahābhārata* refers to the hermitage of Vyāsa, the son of Satyavati. The Vyāsa *Saṁhitā* places the hermitage at Benaras,[1] while the *Pārāśara Saṁhitā* locates it in the *Devadāru* forest on the peak of the Himalayas.[2] *Purāṇa* locates this hermitage on the Alakanandā river which flows past the *Viśāla Badri* peak. But it is possible that the Badri refers to Ādibadri in Ambala district.

Vyāsa who is famous as the author of the *Mahābhārata* had amongst his pupils Summanta, Vaiśampāyana, Jaimini and Paila. Later on they were joined by Śuka, the son of Vyāsa himself. Vyāsa is said to have taught the *Mahābhārata* to Vaiśampāyana, who recited it at the *Sarpa-yajña* of Janmejaya. The *Vyāsa Saṅhitā* refers to the questions asked by sages upon the duties of the different *Varṇas* and embodies the answers to it. *Pārāśara Saṅhitā* also mentions that Vyāsa was asked by the sages to relate to them the rules of good conduct. Vyāsa, well versed in *Śrutis* and *Smṛtis*, took them to his father Parasara's hermitage at

---

1 *Purāṇa*, (1960), Vol. II, Nos.1-2, Varanasi, All India Kashiraj Trust.

2 Das, S.K., (1930), op.cit., pp.319-20.

Badrikā. Parāśara replied to the questions of the sages which are embodied in the *Pārāśara Saṁhitā.*[1]

56. *Hermitage of Yāja and Upayāja.*

The *Mahābhārata* locates the hermitage on the banks of Yamunā and Gaṅgā[2]. It states that king Drupada visited the hermitage while roaming along the banks of these rivers in search of a yajña priest (*Ṛtvija*). He contacted Yāja as directed by Upayāja and requested him to perform the yajña for him which could bestow on him a brave son. Drupada explained to the sage his enmity with Droṇa who is skilled in the use of *Brahma* weapon also and had overcome in a contest. Since Droṇa possesses the *Kṣ atriya* might of the Kurus, he wished to be aided by his *Brahma* force, so that he obtains a son invincible in battle and capable of slaying Droṇa. He offered to give him eighty thousand kine for the purpose. Yāja agreed to perform the *yajña* and *Upayāja* told the king about the things required for the *yajña.* He assured him that a son will be born to him with great prowess and strength.

57. *Hermitage at Ajapālanigrodha.*

---

1 Ibid.

2 Roy, P.C., *op.cit.,* Vol.I (II Ed.), pp. 383-385

According to *Vinaya Piṭaka* the hermitage was located under the banyan tree under which the Buddha sat in deep meditation for a week after his enlightenment[1]. It was here that the Buddha resolved to preach his knowledge. According to Āchārya Buddhaghoṣa, the tree was called *ajapāla* as the goat herds sat under it. It was here that Sujātā served food to Buddha.

58. ***Hermitage of Aśoka.***

This hermitage according to the *Jātakas* was situated near *Himavān* mountains in *Uttarāpatha*[2]. It was built by Visakammā (Viśvakarmā) in the time of Sumedha Buddha.

59. ***Hermitage of Bodhisattva.***

The *Losaka Jātaka* mentions a Bodhisattva teacher of world-wide fame in Benaras[3]. He had five hundred young *Brāhmaṇas* as his pupils who received education at this hermitage. The poor pupils were given food by the people of Benaras. In the *Tīthra Jātaka,* it is mentioned that a renowned teacher of Benaras gave instructions in science to five hundred young *Brāhmaṇas.* One day he decided to retire into

---

1 Bajpai, K.D. *et.al.* (Ed.) (1967)), *op.cit.*, pp.10-11.
2 Ibid., .36
3 Das, S.K. (1930), *op.cit.,* pp.170-171.

a forest onto the slopes of the Himalayas to carry on the teaching there as he saw hindrances to his religious life and the studies of the pupils at Benaras. He told his pupils to bring Sesame, husked rice, oil, garments etc. in the forest hermitage. His pupils also constructed their huts near by the abode of the *Guru* close to the highway. The king-folk of the pupils, natives of the country, and the foresters presented gifts of rice, cow etc. paying homage to the learned scholar.

60. ***Hermitage of Aurva.***

The hermitage of Aurva, a Bhārgava, is mentioned in the *Brahmāṇḍa Purāṇa*[1], *Brahma Purāṇa*[2], *Harivañśa*[3], *Vāyu Purāṇa* and *Śiva Purāṇa*[4]. The story goes that Kārtavīrya had grandsons through Jayadhvaja who were called Tāla Jaṅghas and Vītihotras. To escape from Paraśurāma, the Tāla Jaṅghas retired to the Himalayas. Tālajaṅghas returned to their capital and resumed kingship. They attacked Ayodhyā which was then ruled by Bāhu, the aged father of Sagara. Bāhu fled along with his pregnant wife to the forest and stayed in the vicinity

1 *Brahmāṇda Purāṇa*, Ch-48.

2 *Brahma Purāṇa*, 8. 35-51.

3 *Harivaṁśa*, 14,1029.

4 *Śiva Purāna*, VII, 61, 29-43. J. R.A.S. (1919), 353 ff., Sagara and Haihayas of E.E. Pargitar, and Journal of the Asiatic Society, Vol. iv, no. 2 (19620).

of Aurva's hermitage. He died there due to old age and weakness. His queen who erected the funeral pyre wanted to commit suicide. But Aurva took pity on the pregnant woman and brought her into his hermitage where she gave birth to Sāgara. Sāgara was brought up, taught the Vedas and bestowed the Paraśurāma fire weapon by the sage Aurva. Then Sāgara collected a huge army and conquered the Haihayas and Talajaṅghas and destroyed the forces of Śakas, Yavanas, Kambojas, Pāradas and Pahlavas[1].

61. ***Hermitage of Durvāsā.***

The hermitage of Durvāsā is located in the snowy mountain according to the *Mārkaṇḍeya Purāṇa*[2]. B.C.Law locates it on the highest peak of a hill called *Khallipāhād* to the north of Colgong in the district of Bhagalpur and to the south of Patharjhata[3].

The story goes that once Nārada visited Indra. The latter asked the sage to tell which of the dancers among Rambhā, Karkaśā, Urvaśī, Tillottamā, Chritacī, or Menakā pleased him the most. The sage told him that one who is capable of disturbing the austerities of Durvāśā is the foremost among them. All the dancers declined thinking the task impossible among them. An *Apsarā* named Vapu took the job

---

1 *Purāṇa* (1966), Vol.v iii, No.1, p.58.

2 Pargiter, F.E. (1969), *Mārkaṇḍeya Purāṇa*, Delhi, pp.405.

3 Law, B.C., (1976), *op.cit.*, p.217.

and went to the hermitage of Durvāsā. Durvāsā was filled with anger by seeing her there with a view to perturb him. The sage cursed the *Apsarā* that she will be born in the foolish race of the birds for sixteen years and will give birth to four sons and will be absolved of the guilt by dying in the field of the battle[1].

62. ***Hermitage of Gālava.***

According to the *Bṛhat Śiva Purāṇa* the hermitage was situated on the C*hitrakūṭa* mountain[2]. Gālava is said to have performed penances here. He was famous sage well versed in Vedic lores. B.C. Law has identified the hermitage with a spot three miles away from Jaipur in Rajasthan[3].

63. ***Hermitage of Kapila.***

According to B.C. Law this hermitage is situated in the *Sāgara* island near the mouth of the Ganges[4]. The hermitage is mentioned by *Yoginitantra*[5] and the *Bṛhat Dharma Purāṇa*[6]. Kapila performed penances at this place and was visited by many sages.

64. ***Hermitage of Kardama.***

---

1 Pargiter, F.E. (1969), *op.cit.*, p.5.

2 *Bṛhat Śiva Purāṇa*, Ch.I, 83.

3 Law, B.C., (1976), op.cit., p.316.

4 Ibid., p.224.

5 *Yogini Tantra*, 2.9., pp.214 ff.

6 *Brihat Dharma Purāṇa*, Ch.22.

The hermitage was situated at Siddhapura in Gujrat and according to B.C. Law[1], here lived well known *Ṛṣi* Kardama who performed penances for obtaining liberation.

65. ***Hermitage of Sandīpanī.***

According to the *Bhāgavata Purāṇa*, the hermitage of sage Sandīpanī was located at Avanti (Ujjaini). Krishna having killed Kañśa placed Ugrasena on the throne of Mathura. Consequently the Yadus, Vṛṣṇis, Andhakas, Madhus, Dasrahas and Kukkuras, who had left Mathura for fear of Kañśa returned back. Vasudeva got the *upanayana* of his children performed by his *Purohita* Garga. Krishna and Balarāma went to reside with sage Sandīpanī to learn the *Vedas* and practise asceticism. There also came Sudāmā, a poor *Brāhmaṇa* boy from Kāśī. The two brothers learned the *Vedas. Vedāṅgas* and all branches of knowledge in sixty four days and requested to their guru to ask for his *Dakṣinā*[2].

66. ***Hermitage at Arbunda.***

The hermitage at Arbunda has been identified with the Abu mountain, 17 miles away from Abu Road[3].

---

1 Law, B.C., (1976), op.cit.

2 *Sinha*, Purendu Narayan, (1950), *Bhāgavata Purāṇa*, II Ed., Madras, pp.437-38.

There is a lake on the mountain described by the Jains as Abbuya. Abu is one of the sacred hills of the *Jains.* In addition to Śatruñjaya, Sānnet, Sikhara, Girnār and Candragiri[1], the hermitage of Vaśisṭha[2] and the shrine of the goddess Amba Bhavānī were also located at mount Abu.

67. ***Hermitage of Bhairavācārya.***

Bāṇa in his *Haṛsha-Charita* refers to the hermitage of Bhairavācārya situated near the city of Thanesvara near the bank of Sarasati river[3]. The sage is said to be a second over-thrower of Dakṣa's *yajña.* He was famous for his power and excellence in science. King Puṣpabhūti is known to have visited this hermitage.

68. ***Hermitage of Divākaramitra.***

The *Harṣacarita* of Bāṇa[4]refers to the hermitage of Divākaramitra and locates it in the Vindhya hills[5]. Originally Divākaramitra was a follower of *Maitrāyaṇī śākhā* of the *Vedic* religion. But later on he became a Buddhist and played a part in the conversion of Harṣa and his sister into Buddhism.

---

3 Bajpai, K.D., et. al. (Ed.), (1967), *op.cit.,* pp.31-32.

1 Dey, *op.cit.*, p.10.

2 *Mbh.* 111.82, 555 p., Adi.24.

3 Das, S.K., (1930), op.cit., pp.323-24.

4 *Harṣa Carit,* Cowell and Thomas (Eng. Tr.), pp.236-37.

5 Das, S.K., (1930), *op.cit.,* pp.172-73.

The hermitage was in fact a university which admitted pupils differing widely and radically in doctrines and practices. Followers of all possible sects and schools of thought gathered there in a common fellowship in the search of truth. There came *Digambara Jains* (Arhats), *Moskaris (Brahmanical* ascetics), *Śvetāpata* (*Svetāmbara Jains*) *Bhāgavatas*, *Brahmacāris*, *Keśaluñcakas*, *Sāṅkhyas* and *Lokāyatikas*[1]. They all followed their own tenets, raising doubts, giving etymological explanations, disputing and studying[2].

69. ***Hermitage of Gautama Rahugaṇa.***

According to *Śatapatha Brāhmaṇa*[3] an Aikṣvāku prince named Māṭhava conquered the region to the east of Kośala[4]. It is mentioned that the Gangetic territory of Kośala was conquered by Bhāgiratha before Māṭhava acquired the region to its east. In course of colonization of Videha across a river Sadānirā (Modern Gaṇḍhaka) the prince was accompanied by his spiritual priest Gautama Rahugaṇa. It is stated that no *Brāhmaṇa* ever crossed the river Sadānirā in the former times, since

---

1 Vaidya, C.V., *History of Medieval Hindu*, India, Vol.I., p.III.
2 Das, K.S., (1930), *op.cit.*, pp.172-73.
3 *Śatapatha Brāhmaṇa*, 1,4,1.
4 Bhargava, P.L., (1971), *op.cit.*, p.225.

the land was not purified by the Fire god. Māṭhava and Gautam Rahugaṇa caused this region to be burnt. As a consequence many *Brāhmaṇa* went there and brought the region under cultivation which came to be known as Videha. According to the *Purāṇas*, Gautam Rahugaṇa built a hermitage in this country and a town of Jayanta was founded near by the hermitage by Māṭhava.

70. ***Hermitage of Jābāli.***

Bāṇa in his *Kādambarī* refers to the hermitage of sage Jābāli. There lived many sages and pupils engaged in the studies of the *Vedas* and undertaking meditation and *Yoga* practices[1]. The young *Brāhmaṇas* recited the *Vedas* there eloquently, constructed the leafy huts, plastered the courts with paste, engaged in meditation, yoga, making girdles of *muñja*, washing garments of bark, bringing fuel, decorating deer skin, gathering grass, lotus, rosary beads and bamboos. Here they were taught the performance of *Śrāddha* rites and science of yajña according to the *Rāmāyaṇa*. According to *Kādambarī*, the śāstras of right conduct were examined, good books were recited and the meaning

1 Riddings, C.M. (Eng. Trans.) *Kādambarī*, p.38.

of *śāstras* was pondered over in this hermitage. But the precise location of the hermitage is not known[1].

71. ***Hermitage of Jahnu.***

The hermitage was located in eastern India at Sultanganj in the west of Bhagalpur according to B.C. Law[2]. The temple of Goginātha Mahādeva is said to be situated on the site of the hermitage today. There are several stories connected with the name Jahnu.

72. ***Hermitage at Kukkuṭarāma.***

The Ancient heritage and a monastery of this name is said to be located in the south-east of Patliputra. Aśoka is known to have constructed it after he adopted Buddhism[3].

73. ***Hermitage of Jayasena.***

Hiuen-Tsang refers to the hermitage of Jayasena on the *Yaṣṭivana* hill[4]. Jayasena was a *Kṣatriya* of Surata and lived as a householder on the *Yaṣṭivana* hill. Hiuen-Tsang stayed with him. Jayasena was a writer of *śāstras.* In his young age, he first studied

---

1 Das, S.K., (1930), op.cit., pp.324-25.

2 Law, B.C., (1976), *op.cit.*, p.223; Sharma, J.S., (1972), op.cit., p.85.

3 *Ibid.*, p.106.

4 Das, S.K., (1930), *op. cit.,* pp.171-72.

under Bhadraruchi and then under Sthirmati-Bodhisattva. He studied Śabdavidyā belonging to the *Mahāyāna* and *Hīnayāna.* He learnt *Yogaśāstra* under Śīlabhadra. Then he read numerous productions of secular writers, the four *Vedas*, works on astronomy, geography, medicine, art, magic, arithmetic and about roots and branches of various texts.

Puraṇavarmā, the king of Magadha, was known for respecting the learned men and distinguished sages. Hearing of the fame of Jayasena, the king sent messengers to invite him to come to his court and donated the revenue of twenty large towns for his support. But the learned scholar declined. He was also invited by king Śilāditya who assigned the revenue of eighty large towns of Orissa to him. But the scholar again declined saying that his object was to teach the urgent character of fetters of birth and death. And it was not possible for him to find the leisure to acquaint with the concern of the king[1].

74. *The hermitage at Lahore.*

S.K. Das identifies the hermitage mentioned by Hiuen-Tsang with a forest near Lahore. The Chinese pilgrim mentioned that there lived a *Brāhmaṇa* who looked thirty years of age. His

---

1 Ibid.

understanding was divine and his reasoning power was perfect. He had thoroughly studied the C*handa* and *Piṅgala śāstra*. He was an eminent scholar of the *Vedas* and other works and had two followers. Hiuen-Tsang stayed in his hermitage for one month studying the *Sūtras*, *Śataśāstra*, *Śataśāstra-Vaipulyam* written by Deva Bodhisattva a disciple of Nāgārjuna[1].

75. *Hermitage of Vṛṣaparvā.*

The hermitage was located near the Gandhamādana *parvata* which formed a part of the Rudra Himalaya. But according to the epics, the mountains formed a part of the Kailāśa range[2].

---

1 Das, S.K., (1930), Ibid., p.35.

2 Law, B.C., (1976), *op.cit.*, p.135; Sharma, J.S., (1972), *op.cit.*, p.192.

CHAPTER-3

LIFE IN THE HERMITAGES

1

The earliest reference to the hermitages found in the *Śatapatha Brāhmaṇa*[1] and the *Āraṇyakas* and the *Upaniṣads* pertains to the forest life[2]. These hermitages constituted the schools for imparting spiritual education, training in rituals and in cultivating self discipline. The sages and pupils lived together. They gathered fruit and fuel, grazed their cattle and cultivated spiritual knowledge. The students are mentioned as fetching fuel, keeping fire, begging alms and tending cattle in the *Chhāndogya Upaniṣad.* The study of *Vedas* was one of the vital duties of the pupils. The *Chhāndogya Upaniṣad* enjoins that the pupil would study the *Vedas* in the family of the preceptor after finishing all the duties. The hermits, who were the moral and spiritual preceptors, were also incharge of general education. The natural environment suited to their creative thinking[3].

The interest in the world disappeared in the *Upaniṣ ads*, while in the *Ṛgveda* the *Ṛṣis* lived as households propitiating the gods natural forces with *yajña* and prayers.

---

1 Max Müller, F. (Ed.). *The Sacred Books of the East*, Vol. XII, *Śatapatha Brāhmaṇa*, Tr. by Eggeling.

2 Dewan Bahadur K. Krishnaswami, Rao, (1941). *Endowment Lectures in the Uniersity of Madras.*

3 Chatterjee, Chinmoy, (1957). *Vedantic Education,* Lucknow, pp.14-55.

In the *Ṛgveda* they prayed for family happiness, heroic sons, long and successful life. They had not abandoned their interest in the worldly life. But the sages of the *Upaniṣ ad* took to the life of the forests, away from the hum-drum of the cities and towns. Many of them lived with their families and had children. But this mode of life of the Ṛṣis seems to have ended with the *Purāṇas*[1].

The main objectives of education in this age were to cultivate knowledge, obedience and patience, to inculcate self-control, life of austerity, reverence to authority and respect for tradition. Apart from meditation and a life of simplicity, the students were taught to be hospitable and courteous.

II

The hermitages, according to the *Rāmāyaṇa*, were located in the forests by the side of rivers or lakes both in the plains as well as in the hills. The surroundings of the hermitages were full of trees, plants, flowers and grasses. The landscape was picturesque and provided a feast to the eyes. The natural beauty and calmness would make the hermitage an ideal retreat for those who liked to live away from the turmoil of cities and villages. The lakes were full of lotuses and the trees were laden with fruits and flowers. The *Rāmāyaṇa* gives a vivid description of natural

---

1 Introduction by Sarvapalli Radha Krishnan, (1958) in *The Cultural Heritage of India*, Vol.I, Calcutta, pp.210-13.

surroundings of hermitages at *Pañchvaṭī*[1] in the *Daṇḍakāraṇya*[2] and of the *Saptajanas*[3].

The forests and lakes which formed the surroundings of the hermitages were the natural habitats of wild beasts, deer, swans, water fowls, geese and peacocks, etc., as mentioned in the description of hermitages of Pañchvaṭī, Niśākara[4], Agastya[5], Vālmīki[6], etc. Around the hermitage of Niśakara roamed the wild beasts, such as bears, tigers, lions and snakes. Herds of elephants and deer moved about near the Chitrakūṭa hill.

A variety of trees are mentioned in the *Rāmāyaṇa* as providing the natural environment for the hermitage at *Pañchvaṭī*[7]. These included the trees of *Sāla, Tamāla,* Kharjūra, Plaāśa, *Nivāra, Śirīṣa Punnāgā, Aśoka, Tilaka, Ketaka, Champaka, Syandana, Chandana, Aśhvakarṇa, Khadira, Shami, Tinḍuka, Paṭala, Dhāra*, etc.

---

1 Shastri, H.P., (1969), *The Rāmāyaṇa of Vālmīki,* Vol.II, (Āraṇyakāṇḍa) London, pp.34-35; Sharma, J.S., (1972), *The national Geographical Dictionary of India,* I Ed., New Delhi, p.140; Ed. By Bajpai, K.D. et.al., (1967), *The Geographical Encyclopaedia of Ancient and Medievai India, Part I, Varanasi, p.6.*

2 Shastri, H.P., (1969), *op.cit.*, pp.3-4.

3 *Ibid.*, pp.198-200.

4 *Ibid.*, pp.311-12; Misar Ramgopal, (1951), *Tapo Bhūmi* (Hindi),pp.184-188.

5 Shastri, H.P., (1969), *op.cit.*, pp.27-30.

6 Shastri, H.P., (1962), *The Rāmāyaṇa of Vālmīki*, Vol.I, London, pp.301-303.

7 Shastri, H.P., (1969), *op.cit.*, pp.34-35.

The hermitages were built at suitable spots where the basic nessesities of life could be easily procured and the hum-drum of the village folk or the towns did not distract the sages from their penances and their religious practices. The type of spot considered as the most suitable for hermits dwellings is well described in the *Rāmāyaṇa* when Rāma asked Lakṣmaṇa to find out a place at Pañcavaṭī, which would have the necessary wood, water, fuel, flowers, kuśa-grass etc.

The place should be sufficiently away from the constant disturbance of the cities and towns. In fact Rāma rejected the abode at the hermitage of Bharadvāja[1] for its proximity to Ayodhyā. The first place which was preferred by Rāma for settling down was Chitrakūṭa[13] which was full of roots and fruits and was clean.

The hermitages were distinguished by huts constructed of branches of trees, bamboos, grasses and leaves according to the *Rāmāyaṇa.* Reeds and leaves were used for roof of the huts, while their floors were levelled and covered with *Kuśa-grass*[2]. Some of the hermitages had a number of huts arranged in circles. The huts sometimes had more than one chambers, called *parṇakuṭī* and *uṭaja.* The idea of a hut in the hermitage could be had from Vālmiki's description of Rāma's *parṇasālā* at Pañcavaṭī[3].

---

1 Shastri, H.P., (1962). *Op.cit.*, London, pp. 275-98.
2 Ibid., pp.301-303.
3 Shastri, H.P., (1969). o*p.cit.*, pp.34-35.

The hut was very spacious and the earth was levelled to make the flooring. A soft *kuśa-grass* was spread over the floor. The roof was made of bamboos covered with *Śamī* twigs and fastened with strong ropes. It was finally stuffed and thatched with *Kuśa, Kāsa* and *Śara* blades and leaves.

A hermits' colony was also known as *tapovana.* The hermitages had different quarters for *Agni* or fire, housing the *yajña* fire in the *yajña* dais or *Vedis* and the guests as known from the description of the hermitages of Pañcavaṭī and Bharadvāja[1]. Separate places were set apart for the worship of the gods, the *Caityas* and the Vedis for offering oblations. The courtyards were kept clean and well-swept.

A hermitage was headed by a patriarch sage. Under his spiritual guidance, there resided a host of disciples and recluses, who had renounced the world and devoted themselves to religious duties. The hermits' colonies presented a picturesque sight with costs of bark hanging around, Kuśa-grass spread, deer reclining in shade, birds nestling in branches of trees, sacrificial utensils, water cans, offerings, antelope-skins and *yajña* samidhā being commonly seen there. The hermitages were generally located in the forest which were infested with wild animals and beasts. The tracks were made through the forest by the sages while going for fruit gathering. They marked the

---

[1] Shastri, H.P. (1962). o*p.cit.*, pp.275-98.

trees on the way with Kuśa-grass and bark lest they might lose their way back to hermitage as noticed at Chitrakūṭa[1].

The life in the hermitages was quite disciplined. The hermits mainly lived on roots and fruits obtained from the forest. They had to practice moderation in food and be contented with the edibles from the forest. They were frequently required to observe fast. They avoided flesh and ate only twice a day in the morning and the evening. They also collected grains. Cows were the main source of property. Vaśisṭha is described allegorically as being possessed of Kāmadhenu[2] cow.

There are references in the *Rāmāyaṇa* to the possession of powerful bows and arrows and swords by some of the sages. Agastya[3] is said to have possessed a divine bow encrusted with gold and diamonds, inexhausted quivers filled with sharp arrows, a mighty silver scaffard and a sword decorated with gold. But the hermits perhaps got these in hermitage and passed these on as gifts to the deserving disciples.

The hermits obtained their fuel by hewing wood from the trees. They collected heaps of fuel in the hermitages. The dry dung of cows and deer was also used as fuel.

---

1 *Ibid.*, pp.301-03.
2 Sen, R.R., (1909), *The Triumph of Vālmīki*, Chattong, pp. 7-10.
3 Shastri, H.P., (1969). *op.cit.*, pp.27-30.

The nature of hermit's property was simple and utilitarian. An idea of this can be best had from a reference in the *Rāmāyaṇa* to the gifts made to Lava and Kuśa in Vālmiki's[1] hermitage by the hermits pleased by their recitation of the *Rāmāyaṇa*. The articles thus presented included seats made from udumbara wood, darbha-grass and plaited grass, thread for tying up the mated locks, pitcher, skin of the black deer, water *kāmaṇḍalu*, *kaupina* (lower garment), axe, a girdle of muñja grass, *yajña sūtra* or holy thread and *yajña-bhāṇḍa* or utensils for yajña. The Daṇḍaka forest[2] hermitage also mentioned the skins and jars of water among the objects of use in the hermitages.

The hermits wore minimum required dress which was simple and made of material obtained from forest. They covered themselves up in fibres of *Kuśa-grass*, skin of black deer and bark of valkala which comprised upper and lower garments. *Kaupina* constituted their under garment. They wore matted locks of hair on their heads.

The hermitages had a unique decorum and culture. The hermits were expected to maintain gravity of behavior and the attitude of casualness was discouraged. Even the royal visitors to the hermitages could not violate the decency of the life of the hermitage. When Rāma entered the hermitage of Atri[3] he unstrung his bow. Again,

---

1 Shastri, H.P., (1959). *op.cit.*, pp. 530-32, 568-69, 610-11.

2 Shastri, H.P., (1969). *op. cit.*, pp. 3-4

3 Shastri, H.P., (1962). *op. cit.*, pp. 431-37.

Bharata, while going to see Bharadvāja[1], went on foot along with his ministers. He left the royal retinue behind so that it did not disturb the calm and quite atmosphere of the hermitage. The pious atmosphere of the hermitage chastened the untruthfulness and removed the weakness of the body and mind. Cruelty, craftiness, falsehood and unrighteouness were kept at bay by the spiritual force of these hermitages.

The sages were notorious for their short temper. They would curse anyone for offending their sharp sensibility. But this was the optimum limit of revengefulness and violence. They abhored physical violence.

The culture of the hermitage was marked for hospitality to guests. The traditional mode of entertaining the guests was to offer them water to wash the hands and feet, a seat to sit and food to eat. Guests were also offered Madhuparka, a special preparation which consisted of a mixture of curd, butter, honey and the milk of the coconut. *Bhāradvāja*[2] offered Madhuparka to Rāma and his party. They were also offered the variety of preparations made out of roots and fruits of the forest. The sages looked to the royal guests for protection and showered on them all courtesies befitting the traditional mode of the hermits as at *Daṇḍakāraṇya*[3]. For entertaining the ladies accompanying

---

1 *Ibid.*, pp. 275-98

2 Shastri, H.P., (19462). *op. cit.*, pp. 275-98.

the royal personalities, the wives of the sages attended on them. In the hermitage of Atri[1], Sītā was welcomed by *Anusuya.* When Rāma went to the hermitage of Agastya[2], the sage embraced him and honoured him with water and seat and greeted him according to the traditional mode of the hermitages by offering oblation into the fire and giving arghya and food to the guest. He later made a gift of the celestial bow and arrow and sword to Rāma. The guests were led by the pupils to the patriarch after obtaining his permission. Some of the guests visiting the hermitages offered gifts of food to the hermits, as noticed at *Riṣ yaśriṅga*'s[3] hermitage. There existed retiring rooms (huts) for the guests as at the hermitage of Bhāradvaja[4].

The Royal visitors enquired the sages of their welfare and about their religious practices and distributed gifts to the hermits and the students comprising of necessities of life. Besides, the sage as well as their disciples visited the different hermitages frequently and maintained cordial relations among themselves and exchanged their ideas freely.

---

3 Shastri, H.P., (1969). *op. cit.*, pp. 3-4.
1 Shastri, H.P., (1962). *op. cit.*, pp. 431-37
2 Shastri, H.P., (1969). *op. cit.*, pp. 27-30.
3 Shastri, H.P., (1962). *op. cit.*, pp. 27-28.
4 Ibid., pp. 275-98.

The life of the hermits was quite hard. Their daily routine was largely occupied with the performance of various rites. They bathed thrice a day. In the morning the sages performed their ablutions in the rivers or lakes and adored the Sun with water and returned back to their hermitages with water pots on their shoulders. The hermits observed the rules of their order by performing *yajña* and by reciting the *Vedas*. They offered flowers on the altars, performed Agnihotra and other rituals prescribed by the scriptures. The *bali* (part of food shared by Āśra mites was offered to animals surrounding them, while *homa* was performed to nourish the environment. The *Svādhyāya* and *Agnihotra* were included in the normal routine of the hermits. Then began the schooling of the disciples. A variety of subjects related to religion, philosophy and science were discussed. The main objectives which motivated the hermits to take resort to a life of forest was the performance of penances or meditation. A variety of austerities, methods of self mortification, self restraint and self denial were observed with a view to purify oneself. The hermits observed strict piety, regular study of *Vedas*, moderation in food, control of senses, meditation, righteousness, purity of conduct and honesty. They largely depended upon the products of the forest and observed frequent fasts.

Chitrakūṭa was eminently suited place for penances. The description of Rāma's visit to Janasthāna[1] acquaints us of the multifarious austerities undertaken by the hermits. Some of these hermits lived on raw food, others refused to avail of leisure, some lived under the open sky, some wore wet clothes, while others lived on water or leaves. Some of the hermits were engaged in chanting the *mantras*, other lay in neck deep waters, some lived on high altitudes, while others practised *pañcāgni* penance by sitting in between fires on all four sites at noon. Thus the hermits cultivated peace, steadfastness, mental poise and meditation through various yogic practices.

The hermits in the *Vānaprastha* stage of life were accompanied by their wives. The Bālakāṇḍa refers even to women hermits such as Anasuyā, wife of *Atri*,[1] *Śavarī*[2] and others. They were known for their penances and life of austerities. Śavarī and Svayaṁprabhā, respectively known as *Tāpasī* and *Śarmaṇī*, had renounced the household life for the life of forest. They wore garments of bark of trees and deer skins and had matted locks of hair. They are stated to be over engaged in a life of self-restraint, righteousness, pious observances and devout meditation.

The sages expected people to observe rules of good conduct. In cases of breach of these rules, they were prone to curse the offenders. Agastya[3], Gautama[4], Viśvāmitra[5]

---

1 *Ibid.*, pp. 429-30.

1 *Ibid.*, pp. 431-37.

2 Shastri, H.P., (1969), *op.cit.*, pp. 156-158.

3 *Ibid.*, pp 27-30.

4 Shastri, H.P., (1959), *op.cit.*, pp.475-78.

Vaśiṣṭha[1] and Durvāsā[2] were all known for their hard temperament and cursing habits.

The hermitages gave protection and provided resting place to passers-by at night and other human beings who had no other protection in society. Sītā, when renounced by Rāma, reached the hermitage of Vālmīki[3] and gave birth to Lava and Kuśa there. Vālmīki acted as a god father to Sītā and the two children. The hermitage of Bhāradvāja[4] attracted a number of disciples for receiving education. But the main purpose of these hermitages was performance of penance by the hermits to attain the salvation. The sages in *Daṇḍakāraṇya*[5] hermitages performed all sorts of austerities. The hermitages resounded with the chanting of the Vedic hymns and covered with smoke rising from the *yajñas.* In the hermitage of *Agastya*[6] were set up the altars to various deities *i.e. Brahm, Agni, Viṣṇu, Mahendra, Vivasvat, Soma, Bhaga, Kubera, Dhātṛ, Vāyu, Yama, Kārttikeya and Dharma.* The sages squatted cross-legged in *Padmāsana* with ashes besmeared on their bodies and their faces blazing with luster of penances.

The hermitages also served as educational institutions. King Daśaratha is known to have entrusted his

---

5 Shastri, H.P., (1962), *op.cit.*, pp. 66-67.

1 *Ibid.*, pp. 106-108.

2 Pargiter, F.E. (1969), *Markandeya Purāṇa*, Delhi, p.5.

3 Shastri, H.P., (1959), *op.cit.*, pp. 568-69.

4 Shastri, H.P., (1962), *op.cit.*, pp. 275-98.

5 Shastri, H.P., (1969), *op.cit.*, pp. 3-4

6 *Ibid.*, pp. 27-30.

sons, Rāma and Lakṣmaṇa, to sage Viśvāmitra[1] who trained them in appropriate culture and art of warfare, Much discretion was shown by the preceptor in the selection of the disciple. The *Rāmāyaṇa* for example was taught to Kuśa and Lava for being recited. The preceptor was highly revered by the society as well as the pupils since he conferred the highest gift of knowledge. The *Rāmāyaṇa* declares gurus, virtually, to be gods among men.[2]

The *Rāmāyaṇa* refers to several classes of teachers and prechers as Gurus[3], Ācāryas,[4] Kulapatis,[5] Śrotriyas[6], Tāpasas[7] Brahmavādins[8], Upādhyāyas[9], Śikṣakas[10], Parivrajakas[11] etc.[12]. The pupils lived with the gurus or the *Kulapatis* in the hermitages for receiving education in yogic practices, scriptures, rituals etc. The hermitages of Bhāradvāja[13] Agastya[14], Vālmīki[15], Vaśisṭha[16], Viśvāmitra[17]

---

1 Shastri, H.P., (1962), *op.cit.*, pp. 66-67.
2 *Rāmāyaṇa*, 11.30.33
3 *Ibid.*, 11.111.3.
4 *Ibid.*, 11.111.4.
5 *Ibid.*, 11.116.4.
6 *Ibid.*, of. 1.1.1.
7 *Ibid.*, 1.14.12.
8 *Ibid.*, 1.12.5.
9 *Ibid.*, 11.100.14.
10 *Ibid.*, 11.91.18.
11 *Ibid.*, 111.47.1.
12 Venakataswara, S.V., *Indian Culture Through the Ages*, Vol.I,pp.128-30.
13 Shastri, H.P., (1962). *op. cit.*, pp. 275-96.
14 *Ibid.*, pp. 27-30.
15 Shastri, H.P., (1959). *op. cit.*, pp. 568-69.
16 Shastri, H.P., (1962), *op.cit.*, pp. 106-108.
17 *Ibid.*, pp. 60-67

etc. were known for the flocking of disciples for obtaining knowledge.

The hermits or Kulapatis had no fixed income through grants or tuition fees. Some of them received voluntary gifts from the royal patrons or the students when they departed after completing the courses. The royal patrons granted cows and other necessities of life on ceremonial occasions or when they paid visits to the hermitages. The students by tending the cows, collecting fuel, roots and fruits helped the Guru in maintaining his establishment[1] . In a few cases there are references to the cattle keeping and cultivation of the fields at the hermitages.

The instruction was planned in tune with the work outlook of the hermitages. The students were taught habits of simple life, discipline, austerity and hardwork. They lived with the preceptor in the hermitage unaffected by the social status of their parents. Even the princes had to abide by the same discipline of austerity[2] as the commoners. The students' life at the hermitages was characterized by self discipline, firm control over the senses, tapa and vow of cetibate life to attain knowledge. The foremost duty of the students was to revere the Guru and obey his commands unhesitatingly. He was expected to behave in conformity with the decorums of the hermitage. He rendered personal

---

1 *Rāmāyaṇa*, 1.52.9 and 11.19.8.

2 *Ibid.*, 1.22.24.

service to the teacher[1] in keeping the hermitage clean, cutting wood for fuel and collecting other sacrificial material necessary for yagña.[2] The students' daily routine began early in the morning by taking bath and performing prayers and sandhyā which were repeated in the evening. The hermitage was the residential seat of learning. It was presided over by the chief hermit or Kulapati. The sages and *munis* lived with their wives[3], sons and daughters. The children obtained the necessary education from their parents.[4] the *Rāmāyaṇa* mentions Rāma visiting many hermitages in course of his exile. At the Bhāradvāja[5] hermitage, the *Rāmāyaṇa* describes the sage being surrounded by batches of pupils who lived in huts on both banks of Yamuna. The evening hours in these hermitages were usually spent in discourses on different topics.[6] Women were also permitted to join these institutions. There is a reference to both male and female pupils in the hermitage of Vālmīki.[7]

The hermits and the pupils occasionally paid visit to other hermitages to interact and augment their knowledge. They visited the royal courts on occasions of learned gathering and festivals. Janaka is known as a great patron

---

1 *Ibid.*, 1.22.23.
2 *Rāmāyaṇa*, 111.1.45.
3 *Ibid.*, VII.49.1.14.
4 *Ibid.*, VII.64.32.
5 Shastri, H.P., (1962). *op.cit.*, pp. 275-98.
6 *Rāmāyaṇa*, 11.54.34.
7 Shastri, H.P., (1959). *op.cit.*, pp. 568-69.

of scholars.[1] Vālmīki and his disciples including Lava and Kuśa attended Rāma's *Aśvamedha.*[2] The roaming hermits and pupils established efficient communication between the hermitages and the people at large.

The method of teaching was oral. It was the cheapest and most efficient. Emphasis was laid on memory to ensure the use of knowledge althrough life. It was this mode of learning which protected the original character of the Vedas and even of the *Rāmāyaṇa.* The popular method of teaching religion and morality was through Kathās (allegorical stories).[3] It made the lessons interesting and brought home the abstract philosophical and ethical concepts otherwise difficult to be understood. Recitation of scriptures in the morning was a common feature in the hermitages.[4] *Svādhyāva* and learned discussions and deliberations were the other important feature of the educational system of the hermitages.

Women were not barred from admission to the hermitages. Some of them continued their studies and penances althrough their lives, others married later. Ahalyā is said to have married her preceptor[5] only. Ātreyī[6], Śavari[7] and Anasūyā[8] were some of the famous women

---

1 *Rāmāyaṇa*, 1.31.

2 *Ibid.*, VII.93.1,4.

3 *Ibid.*, 1.23.22.

4 *Ibid.*, V.59.31.

5 *Ibid.*, VII.30.26-27.

6 Shastri, H.P., (1959), *op.cit.*, pp. 568-69

7 Shastri, H.P., (1969), *op.cit.*, pp. 156-58.

hermits. The education in the hermitages, infact, was open to all sections of society. The chief objective of the hermitages was cultivation of both spiritual knowledge. Only competent and deserving pupils were admitted. The bulk of the students although come from the intellectual and the ruling classes, but the admission of Śavarī shows that even the tribal's and other low castes when adequately motivated for a spiritual goal had no bar in taking to the life of a hermit.

III

The hermitages in the *Mahābhārata* and the later *Sanskrit* literature also reveal a preference for forest. These were located in the plains or the hills on the bank of the rivers and lakes. The groves of coconut trees graced the *Śvetaketu*[1] hermitage. The other hermitages were surrounded with trees bearing fruits and flowers and sweet roots as described in respect of the hermitages of Vaśiṣṭha.[2] Nara and Nārāyaṇa[3], Kaṇva[4] and Dvaitavana.[5]

A variety of deer, birds, peacocks monkeys, bears and even elephants were seen roaming as in case of

---

8 Shastri, H.P., (1962), *op.cit.*, pp. 431-37.

1 Roy, P.C., *The Mahābhārata of Krishna Dvaipayana Vyāsa*, Vol.III, II Ed., Calcutta, pp.281-89.

2 Roy, P.C., *op.cit.*, Vol.I, II Ed., Calcutta, pp. 235-37.

3 Roy, P.C., *op.cit.*, Vol.I, III, II Ed., pp. 308-309.

4 Roy, P.C., *op.cit.,* Vol.I, II Ed., pp.167-168.

5 Roy, P.C., *op.cit.*, Vol.II, II Ed., pp.53-54; S, Kamala, (1965), *Mahābhārata*, Bombay, pp. 190-192.

Dadhīcha[1] and *Kāmyaka*[2] Vana hermitages. The trees mentioned in *Dvaitavana* hermitage include *Sāla, Palm, Mango, Madhuka, Nipas, Kadam, Sarjjas, Arjuna, Karnikāra* etc. The sages studied the Vedas, practised penances and performed allegorical Yajñas as in the *Rāmāyaṇa.* Their aim was to obtain supernatural powers or spiritualism, Two women hermits near Kurukshetra[3] lived the life of celibacy for attaining this goal.

The hermitage of Nara and Nārāyaṇa[4] contained fire altars, sacred ladles, pots, water jars and baskets. In the Bhārdvaja[5] hermitage the room for Agnihotra was a separate one. The hermits lived household's lfe. Parāśara was born in the Vaśisṭha's hermitage[6] and the great sage performed the *sausparas* and ceremonies of his grand son. The killing of Bhāradvāja's son in the Raivya[7] hermitage and the performance of Rākṣasa sacrifice by Parāśara reflect the terrorist like activities within the society.

The Kaṅva's[8] hermitage was known for Vedic studies and meditation. The sages were skilled in the

---

1 Roy, P.C., *op.cit.*, Vol.II, II Ed., pp. 225-26.

2 *Ibid.*, pp. 15-17.

3 Quoted by Das, S.K., (1930), *Educational System of the Ancient Hindus*, Calcutta, p. 322.

4 Roy, P.C., *op.cit.*, Vol.III, II Ed., pp. 308-09.

5 *Ibid.*, pp. 294-95.

6 Roy, P.C., *op.cit.*, Vol.I, II Ed., pp. 410-415.

7 Roy, P.C., *op.cit.*, Vol.III, II Ed., pp. 293-94.

8 Roy, P.C., *op.cit.*, Vol.I, II Ed., pp. 167-168.

correct pronunciation of the mantras, construction of fire altars, code of conduct, logic, science and the knowledge of the Vedas. Some of them were engaged in undertaking austere practices and meditation with a view to attain Mokṣ a as their goal, while others had taken rigid vows of Tapa and Homa. The hermitage of *Śaunaka*[1] was famous for the performance of a twelve year yajña by the Kulapati in the Naimiṣa forest. The Dvaitavana[2] also attracted the sages for austerity and penances and the knowledge of the self.

Some of the hermitages were known for the performance of penances and great Vedic learning of the sages e.g., the hermitage of Jamadagni.[3] A number of them became famous as centres of great learning e.g., the hermitages of Vyāsa[4], Droṇa[5], Gautama Saradvāt[6], Kaṇva[7] and Bhārgava.[8] Vyāsa taught Vedas to his disciples. Jaimini, Paila, Vaiśampāyana and Śuka were some of the famous disciples at the hermitage of this great sage who was well versed in Śrutis (secondary tests composed based upon Śrutis) and Śmṛtis (the texts originated owing to primary expenences of seers).

---

1 *Ibid.*, pp. 1-17.

2 S. Kamala, (1965); *op.cit.*, pp. 190-92; Roy, P.C., *op.cit.,* Vol II, II Ed., pp. 53-54.

3 Roy, P.C., *op.cit.*, Vol.III, II Ed., pp. 254-55.

4 *Mahābhārata*, *Vyāsasaṁhitā* quoted by Das, S.K., (1930), *op.cit.,* pp. 319-20.

5 Roy, P.C., *op.cit.,* Vol. II, II,Ed., pp. 312-16.

6 Roy, P.C., *op.cit.,* Vol. I, II Ed., pp. 303-304.

7 *Ibid.*, pp. 167-68.

8 S.Kamala, (1965), *op.cit.*, pp. 40-50.

The hermitage of Droṇa had attained fame as a centre of the science of arms. Kauravas and Pāṇḍavas became proficient in the art of fighting on horse-back, on elephants, on chariot and on foot under his tutelage. Arjuna learnt fighting with mace, sword, lance, spear and bow and arrow. Besides he obtained Vedic learning as well.

The hermitage of Gautama Saradvāt was also famous for the science of weapons. He taught it to his son Kṛpa, the sons of Dhṛtarāṣṭra, Pāṇḍavas, Yādavas and the Vṛṣṇis. The hermitage of Kaṇva was known for the study of the *Vedas*, grammer, prosody, *Nirukta*, astronomy, allegorical *yajñas* etc. Bhārgava taught the art of archery to Droṇa and Karṇa.

The seekers of knowledge, the hermits or pupils, did not remain confined to a single hermitage. The sages and students moved to different hermitages acquiring specialized knowledge and attending the conferences organized by sages of eminence. Sex morality was highly valued as a virtue by the inmates of the hermitages. It was one of the vows of the hermits and students to lead a life of celebate or *Brahmacārin.* Yet the cases of bigamy, rape and laxity in sex were not altogether unknown. The men of the ruling classes generally indulged in cases of sex laxity when they visited the hermitages. Even the sons of hermits were not free from the sex perversion. Yavakri, the son of

Bhardvāja is known to have seduced the daughter-in-law of Raivya in the latter's hermitage[1] which led to the murder of Yavakri. The wife of Jamadagni was killed by her son Parśurāma on the instructions of his father for such an act. On another occasion the wife of the sage was abducted by the son of Kṛtavīrya which led to the murder of the latter and of Jamadagni[2].

The entertainment of guests, the dress and the rules of conduct at the hermitages do not seem to be much different from the age of the *Rāmāyaṇa* in the *Mahābhārata.*

IV

The hermitages in the seventh century do not seem to be much different from the earlier one's. Bāṇa in his *Kādambarī* describes the hermits or *Munis* and their pupils reciting the Vedas, bringing fuel, Kuśa-grass, flowers and earth at the hermitage of Jābālī[3]. The hermits and pupils constructed their huts, covered these with leaves and smeared the courtyards and the huts with clay. They were busy meditating, uttering mantras, practising *Yoga* and performing *yajñas.* They made their girdles of *muñja* grass, garments of bark and decorated deer skins, brought fuel, gathered grass and dried lotus seeds, strung rosaries and stored bamboos. The hermitage was famous for the teaching and the performance of *Śrāddha* rites, the science

---

1 Roy, P.C., *op.cit.*, Vol.III, II Ed. Pp. 293-94.

2 Roy, P.C., *op.cit.,* Vol.II, II Ed., pp. 254-55.

3 C.M. Ridding (Eng. Trans.), Bana's *Kādambarī,* p. 38

of *yajña* and the study of *Śāstras* and good books of every kind.[1]

Hieun-Tsang refers to the hermitage of Jayasena[2] in the hills of Vastivana. He was a native of Surat and a Kṣ atriya by caste. He was the master of Śabda Vidyā Śāstra, Yogaśāstra, Vedas, works on astronomy, geography, medicinal art, magic and arithmetic. He stayed as a householder and maintained an institution of learning where his disciples learnt the books on Buddhism.

Bāṇa also describes the hermitage of Divākaramitra in the Harṣacharita.[3] The sage Divākaramitra was originally a follower of Vedic religion, but later on he became a Buddhist and played an important role in the conversion of Harṣa and his sister to Buddhism. The hermitage lay in the Vindhyan hills and provided an eclectic environment to the pupils who subscribed to radically different doctrines and practices. They were followers of all possible sects and school of thought gathered together to serve the supreme objective of a university. They included Digambara Jains, Brahmanical ascetics, Śvetāmbara Jains, Bhāgavatas, Brahmacarins, Keśaluñcakas, Kapilas or Sāṅkhyas and Lokāyatikas.[4] They followed their own tenets in the same hermitage.[5]

---

1 Quoted by Das, S.K., (1930), *op.cit.*, pp. 324-25.
2 *Ibid.*, pp. 171-172.
3 Cowell and Thomas, Eng. Trans. Bāṇa's *Harṣacarita*, pp. 236-37.
4 Vaidya, C.V., *History of Medieval Hindu India*, Vol.I, p.111.

The description of these hermitages by Bāṇa shows great diversity in the curriculum and eclectic approach to education in the institutions of higher learning. The pupils were no more expected to abide by the Vedic allegorical rituals and the penances which were a feature of the hermitages of the earlier period. The hermitages now emerged into the universities.

V

The Purāṇas do not indicate much of a difference in the life of the hermitages. The Mārkaṇḍdeya Purāṇa[1] refers to the hermitage of Durvāsā on a snowy mountain, perhaps the Himalayas. The Muni practised penances by controlling his senses.

The *Brahmāṇḍa Purāṇa*[2] relates to the hermitage of Aurva where Sagara was born and brought up by the sage. He was taught the Vedas and bestowed Paraśurāma's fire weapon. Both these instances indicate the performance of austerities by the hermits in the forests. The teaching of the *Vedas* was known but there is no reference to the Vedic rituals. The *Bhāgavata Purāṇa*[3] mentions the hermitage of Sandīpanī. It was located in the city of Avanti (Ujjaini) and was thronged by students from far and wide to learn the

---

5 Quoted by Das, S.K., (1930). *op.cit.*, pp.172-73.

1 Pargiter, F.E., (1969). *Mārkaṇḍeya Purāṇa*, Delhi, pp. 4-5.

2 *Purāṇa* (1966), Vol. VIII, No. 1, All India Kashiraj Trust, p. 58.

3 Sinha, Purnendu Narayan, (1950). *Bhāgavata Purāṇa*, II Ed. Madas, pp. 437-38.

Vedas and *Vedāṅgas* etc. But the hermitages in the *Rāmāyaṇa* and the *Mahābhārata* were located away from the cities and the towns. It seems the educational institutions and the hermitages later on came to be established in towns also.

The hermitage was cooperative experiment. Where there was no subordination to any one. Everyone tried to live an integrated life. While students came to the hermitages to learn theology, literature and the hermits aimed at realizing the higher goal of life. As such, tapa i.e. sustained and intensive spiritual efforts was the primary feature of the hermit's life. The highest knowledge or the spiritual knowledge was imparted to the pupils who were qualified for it in character and capacity.

CHAPTER – IV

THE ORIGIN AND DEVELOPMENT OF THE HERMITAGES

I

The earliest clear description of the hermitages (*Aśramas*) in any detail is met within the *Rāmāyaṇa* and *Mahābhārata* even though the first reference to such an institution occurs in the *Śatapatha Brāhmaṇa*. The accounts continue to be found in the classical Sanskrit literature (see chapter-II). The Sanskrit English Dictionary[1] Describes *Aśrama* as a hermitage or the abode of ascetics, the cell of a hermit or retired saints or sages. Apte[2] also translates the term *Aśrama* in the *Rāmāyaṇa* as a hermitage, hut, cell, dwelling or the abode of ascetics. The hermitage was also called *Tapovana* in the ancient literature which literally meant a forest for penances – as given by Apte, In fact, the hermitage means a place for toil or *tapa* (penance) which constituted the mode of life of the *Vānaprasthas* or *Bhikṣus*. In Indian culture it conveys the picture of the forest where the huts of the ascetics were located. These hermits generally resided on the river or lake-sides in the plains or on the hills and their hermitages were surrounded by groves of trees and beautiful natural landscape.

---

1 Williams, Monier, (1976), *Sanskrit English Dictionary*, p.131.

2 Apte, V.S., (1957), *Sanskrit English Dictionary*, Part I, Poona, p.368

The *Aśrama* word conjures up the picture of an aged *Ṛṣi*, his family and the disciples living together in the forest kindling the sacred fire, wearing the bark of the trees or skin of the deer and collecting the fuel from the wood. The flocks of deer move about unscared. Even the kings dare not disturb their peace. These hermitages were located at places which abounded in water, roots and fruits and provided subsistence for the sages.

An important function of the sages in the hermitages was to practice asceticism by undergoing penances, studying the *Vedas* and performing the daily rituals or Agnihotra. In some of the hermitages the *Vedāṅgas* or military skills were also taught. But only a few of the hermitages specialized in the study of the *Vedāṅgas* and the Military Science.[1] The bulk of the hermitages served as secret forest resorts for undertaking austerities, esoteric practices and meditation leading to self-control and self discipline. The hermits lived mainly on roots and fruits of the forest. These penances helped them in cultivating control of senses and strong will power and in the acquisition of physical and spiritual efficiency. The study of the Vedas, considered as the traditional source of all knowledge, and the performance of the daily rituals in the fire suggests their respect for the Vedic tradition and continuity of the culture of the society. The hermits cultivated humility and entertained their guests in the most

---

1 See Chapter III.

befitting manner ever conceived by a civilized society. They were kind to all creatures and adhered to the virtues of truthfulness, non-violence, non-stealing, non-hoarding and celibacy. But the chief goal of the life of the hermits, however, was self-realization or *Mokṣa*. This shows that the purpose of the hermitages was predominantly spiritual. The Vedic studies and the rituals generally had a subordinate position in their culture. Yet, these represented a cultural continuity of the Vedic tradition and valued these strains in the scheme of life as source of lower knowledge. The spiritual education constituted the higher knowledge. It is in this sense that the *Upaniṣads* use the terms *Aparāvidyā* (physical knowledge) and *Parā vidyā*[1] (metaphysical knowledge). The physical knowledge helped the disciples to earn their livelihood in the world and as such considered essential for crossing the ocean of existence[2].

This, however, does not mean that all the hermitages specialized in the cultivation of spiritual knowledge and the achievement of the ultimate reality. It is possible to visualize a variety of thinkers in the hermitages living at different levels of spiritual attainments. G. C. Pande refers to a number of hermits and thinkers propounding a variety of ideas.[3] Yet they all seem to be committed to the ascetic mode of life and culture.

---

1 *Muṇḍakopaniṣad*, 1.1.4.

2 *Īśa. Up.* 1-11.

3 Pande, G.C., (1974), *The Origins of Buddhism*, Delhi, pp. 310-

II

Although there are no clear direct references to the hermitages in the Vedic literature, the *Āraṇyakas* (Books by forest dwellers) and the *Upaniṣads* (the spiritual knowledge) certainly seem to be the products of the hermitages. The dominant strain in this literature is a life of *tapa*, asceticism and meditation for attaining the goal of Self-realization. The knowledge of the Ultimate Reality was the main theme of the *Upaniṣads*.

The *Āraṇyakas* are chapters in the *Brāhmaṇas* which were either written by the hermits themselves or used by them. They marked a transition of knowledge from physical to metaphysical levels. The complex allegorical rituals demanding construction of the elaborate Vedis (altars) recital of the mantras, find their transition into their symbolic meanings for hermits. They considered the ritual as an insecure boat for crossing the ocean of the world. They enjoyed a life of austerity, meditation and self-control, away from the hum-drum of the towns and cities. By the time of the *Upaniṣads* the goal of comfortely on hermits' life had considerably evolved. Their aim was dominated by the idea of Self-realization. This marked emancipation of thought from ritualism of the *Brāhmaṇas* and the severe asceticism aimed at acquisition of supernatural powers. The philosophical questions relating to nature of the universe, the place of man in it and the

---

368.

relation of man to man and other things around him are now answered differently and the methodology conceived for the attainment of the Ultimate goal is in contrast with the main stream of the Brahmanical thought. These problems are discussed with child-like simplicity through dialogues between the teacher and the pupil. The sacred knowledge also called *Guhiyam* or *Rahasyam* was imparted in secret sessions in the forest to the deserving pupil. The philosophical truths were required to be meditated upon to bring about intellectual conviction. *Śravaṇa, Manana* and *Nididhyāsana* was the method adopted for realizing the truth or Self. The *Upaniṣads*, however, do not teach one single philosophy although *Vedānta* was the dominant theme of this literature. Barua has tried to reconstruct the philosophical views met within the *Āraṇyakas* and the *Upaniṣads*[1]. These included the views of individual philosophers showing broad speculating ideas in circulation as Thibaut has suggested[2]. These were not the creation of any individual mind but the general speculations carried on by generations.

Although the Āraṇyakas and the *Upaniṣads* aimed at the knowledge of the self, the study of the *Veda* and the performance of the simple *Agnihotra* were not neglected. In fact, this was considered essential though part of *Avidyā* (ignorance) leading to Śreyasa (the ultimate wellbeing)

---

1 Barua, B., (1921), *A History of Pre-Buddhistic Indian Philosophy*, xxxiv, Calcutta, pp. 51-187.

2 Thibaut, G. in '*Sacred Books of the East*' Introduction Civ.

only. It was mentioned as *Aparā vidyā* (physical knowledge) which could help only for the wordly existence, the Parā vidyā or (meta physical knowledge) being the knowledge of Ātman or Brahman.

It appears from the above account of the culture of the *Āraṇyakas* and *Upaniṣads* that it was saturated by spiritualism and asceticism as the life of the hermitages in the Epics. The continuity of Vedic tradition in the form of the study of the Vedas and performance of the simple daily rites in the fire were also common between the later Vedic literature and the epics. It appears that both of these breathed more or less the same atmosphere. Besides, there occur several names of the hermits in the *Āraṇyakas* and *Upaniṣads* which are common to the epics. These names include Atri, Gotama, Jamadagni, Bhāradvāja, Bhārgava, Viśvāmitra and Vyāsa etc[1]. The internal evidence of the *Āraṇyakas* and the *Upaniṣads* thus indirectly suggests the existence of hermitages in the *Āraṇyaka* and the *Upanisadic* age.

III

The term *Aśrama* (hermitage) does not occur in the pre-*Upanisadic* literature though we do find terms like *Śramaṇas, Tapasa, Vaikhānasa, Vrātya, Yati, Ṛṣi, Muni* and *Brahmacarin* etc. the term Ṛṣi according to the authors

---

1 Macdonell and Keith, (1958), *Vedic Index of Names and Subjects*, Vols, I and II, Varanasi.

of the Vedic Index, means a seer or a composer of hymns to the gods and first occurs in the *Ṛgveda*[1]. *Ṛgveda*[2] mentions seven Ṛṣis sitting in penances and attaining a direct vision of reality through *Tapasa* (asceticism), literally meaning "heat" and perhaps suggesting some sort of physical or mental torture originally resulting from association with fire with a view to obtain super-natural powers. In the *Bṛhadāraṇyaka Upaniṣad*[3] there is reference to the seven Ṛṣis i.e. Gotama, Bhāradvāja, Visuāmitra, Jamadagni, Vasiṣṭha, Kaśyapa and Atri. The *Atharvaveda*[4] also contains a long list of Ṛṣis.

Tāpasa or ascetic is mentioned in the Vedic literature. The *Pañcaviñśa Brāhmaṇa* describes a Tāpasa who was hotṛ priest at the Sarpa yojña[5].

The term Brahmacārin means a religious student. The term occurs in the *Ṛgveda*[6], *Śatapatha Brāhmaṇa*[7], *Atharvaveda*[8], *Taittirīya Saṅhitā*[9], *Taittirīya Brāhmaṇa*[10] and other later Vedic texts.

---

1 *ibid.*, pp. 115-17.
2 *Ṛgveda*, x 109.4.
3 *Brhadāraṇyaka Upaniṣad*, II.2.6.
4 *Atharvaveda*, IV.29.
5 *Pañcaviñśa Brāhmaṇa*, XXV. 15.
6 *Ṛgveda*, X.109.5.
7 *Śatapatha Brāhmaṇa*, XI.3.3,1.
8 *Atharvaveda*, VI. 108,2; 133, 3; XI.5,1.
9 *Taittirīya Saṅhitā*, VI.3, 10,5.
10 *Taittirīya Br.*, III. 7,6,3.

According to Macdonell and Keith[1] the term *Yati* means the name of an ancient class connected with the Bhṛgus in *Ṛgveda.* It continues to occur in the *Sāmaveda* (II.304), *Atharvaveda* (II.5.3), *Taittirīya Saṁhitā* (II.4,9,2) *Kāṭhaka Saṁhitas* (VIII.5; XI.10; XXV.6; XXXVI.7) and some of the *Brāhmaṇas.* The term *Yati* is of Sanskrit origin and is derived from the root *Yam* (to control). According to Haripada Chakraborty[2] the *Yati* represented a different class of ascetics following more rigorous laws than the *Muni.* But they belonged to the Ṛgvedic period. Their knowledge of cosmic phenomena like Indra is apparent in *Ṛgveda.*

The term *Vrātya* occurs in The *Atharvaveda*[3] for the first time as practising *tapa* and having superanatural vowers of the Gods. Sometimes they are described as wandering in search of food and lodging. A Vrātya was respected by *Brāhmaṇas* and King. The *Pañcaviñśa Brāhmaṇa* mentions the *Vrātyas* as self controlled ascetics.[4] The *Atharva-veda*[5] describes the *Vrātya* as a mendicant of a roving spirit, standing erect for a whole year and having seven *Prāṇas* seven *apānas* and seven *Vyānas*[6].

---

1 Macdonell and Keith (1958), op.cit., Vol.II, p.185.

2 Chakraborty, Haripada (1973), Asceticism in Ancient India, Calcutta, pp.3-14.

3 *Atharva-veda*, XV.2.3.

4 *Pañcaviñśa Brāhmaṇa*, XVII,4.1.

5 *Atharva-veda*, XVI.3.1.

6 Ibid., XV.1.2.

The term *Śramaṇa* occurs only in the later *Vedic* literature. It is derived from the root *Śrama* which means labour or exertion. Hence, one who exerts for knowing reality is Śramaṇa. In other words *Śramaṇa* was an ascetic and owed the vow of chastity. In the *Bṛhadāraṇyaka Upaniṣad* the term Śramaṇa is used with Tāpasa[1]. The *Dīghanikāya*[2] uses Śramaṇa-Brāhmaṇa as a compound and suggests men of equal status labouring for spiritual life. Vānaprasthas were the most honoured Śramaṇas. They lived in the forst on wild fruits and leaves, wear the bark of trees and abstained from sexual indulgence and wine. The *Taittirīyāraṇyaka*[3] uses the term vātarasnā to mean Śramaṇas and Urdhvamanthins. It mentions (I.23) that Arunas, Ketus and Vātarasanās arose from the flesh of the Prajapati. Vāikhanas came out of his nails and Valakhilyas from his hair. These ascetics enjoyed highest pleasure (*unmādita*) on account of penances. They lived at a higher level than the ordinary mortals.

References to munis are met with in the Vedic literature. The *Ṛgveda*[4] describes them as moving through the sky at will, dwelling in both the oceans, following the path of the beasts and celestials in the forest. It describes them as long haired persons upholding fire, moisture, heaven and earth.[5] Indra is prayed in the *Ṛgveda*,

---

1 *Bṛhadāraṇyaka Upaniṣad*, IV.3.22.

2 *Dīghanikāya*, I.30.

3 *Taittirīyāraṇyaka*, II.7.

4 *Ṛgveda*, X,135.2 and 136

5 *Ibid.*, VII.56.8.

(VIII.3.5) to be friendly with munis. The *Atharva-veda* also refer to the divine muni as the master of supernatural power obtained through ascetic performance.[1] They are also described as vātarasnā. They wore yellow and soiled clothes and moved along the wind. They obtained the status of the gods. The term vātarasnā perhaps means one having wind as his girdle i.e., nacked.

The *Ṛgveda* also refers to Keśin[2]. He was an ascetic with long hair according to Sayana. He became full of effulgence and identified with fire, wind and sun by the performance of tapa or asceticism.

Thus there is ample evidence to believe that the Vedic literature, both the early and the later Vedic, has reference about the prevalence of asceticism. The Brāhmaṇas on the one hand and the munis, yatis, Vrātyas, Vaikhanas, Brahmacarins, Srāmanas, Vālkhilyas and Ṛṣis on the other hand point to distinct religious paths in the Vedic literature. Rhys Davids points out that the goal of *yajña*, the chief concern of the Brāhmaṇas was to attain worldly power, wealth, children and heaven. While the *tapa* (asceticism) was aimed at attaining mystic, extra-ordinary superhuman faculties. Even the gods were supposed to have practised Tapa to create the world. The asceticism thus involves elements of magical practices. The

---

1 *Atharvaveda*, VII.74.1.

2 Macdonell and Keith, (1958), op.cit.

main strain of the *Rgveda*, later *Saṁhitās* and the *Brāhmaṇas* was unmistakably positive and wordly.

The study of the veda and performance of Vedic sacrifices were pre-dominantly important in the early Vedic society. The later Vedic age is marked by the further growth of conservative thinking reflected in the elaboration of the Vedic rituals and emphasis on the correct pronunciation, and correct understanding of the meaning of the veda. The six vedangas developed for the proper study of the Veda, accurate performance of the sacrifice and for exact calculations of the time of the rituals.

Thus the teaching of the Veda and the performance f the rituals reflected the values of the dominant sections and influenced all sections of the society. The ascetics could not have remained immune to the ideals of the society even for their worldly existence.

It is significant that some of the names of rsis mentioned in the Rgveda and the later Vedic literature occur in the epics as well. The list of the names of the rsis is given in Appendix V. This marks a continuity in the tradition from the Rgveda to the epics and helps in projecting the ascetic mode of life into later Vedic from the RgVedic times. Perhaps the rudiments of the hermitage culture had already emerged as early as the RgVedic age.

IV

The question whether the ascetic tradition in the Vedic culture was indigenous or it had a non-Vedic genesis has been greatly debated among scholars. Dr. Sukumar Dutt[1] is of the view that the institution of religious mendicancy was non-Vedic in origin. The main reasons for considering the Śramaṇic tradition as non-Vedic is that the Śramaṇas did not appeal to the Vedic authority. They did not value the Yajñopavita and shaved their hair and beard. The Vedic authority, the sacred thread and the long hair were the essential marks of the Vedic culture. Professor G. C. Pande also traces the origin of Buddism and other ascetic sects to the Sramaṇic tradition.[2] According to him the Vedic tradition originally recognized only two *Aśramas*. The influence of primitive thought attaching sanctity to the forests and hills led to the growth of asceticism in the Vedic fold. The ideal of asceticism was adopted by Jains and Buddhists not from the *Brāhmaṇas*, but from previously existing heretical ascetic sects.

On the other hand Jacobi, R.G. Bhandarkar[3] and H. Dutta Sharma have suggested Vedic origin of the ascetic tradition[4]. According to him, *pravṛtti* and *nivṛtti* were not the products of distinct cultures but originated in the Vedic-fold itself. Monasticism is also found in the Greek culture. The Greek word 'monos' corresponds with the Sanskrit

---

1 Dutt, Sukumar, *Early Buddhist Monachism*, pp.60-63.

2 Pande, G.C. (1974), op.cit., pp. 310-61.

3 *Ibid.*, pp. 310-61

4 Sharma, H.D., (1939), *History of Brahmanical Asceticism*, vol.III, No.4. Poona.

word 'muni' and means "along" and "solitary".[1] Hence, asceticism which represented a form of religious life led by those who renounced the world and lived in solitude in the other Indo-European societies as well. The Jain work Uttarajjhan[2] mentions how the sight of a man taken for execution and the cry of the animals being killed for marriage ceremony evoked pity in the minds of the sensitives and induced them to leave this worldly life.

Yet Rhys Davids divides ascetics into many classes.[3] the Kalpasūtras, however, distinguished between orthodox and the heterodox ascetics.[4] According to Kane these ascetics differed mainly in their attitudes to the caste system and the scriptures.[5] The above evidence of an ascetic was not confined to the Brahmanical culture alone.

An interesting light on the origin of asceticism is thrown by the evidence of small objects such as three seals from Mohenjodaro and a number of terracotta human figurines from the Indus sites. These Mohenjodaro seals represent a three faced male figure wearing horned head dress and seated in a Yogic pose on throne with crossed legs, hand stretched and the eyes concentrated on the tip of the nose. The figure is surround by wild animals like the

---

1 *Ibid.*

2 Tr. by Jacobi, *Sacred Books of the East*, Vol.45, pp. 108, 109 and 114.

3 Rhys Davids (1936), *The Birth of Indian Psychology and its Development in Buddhism*, pp. 144-6.

4 *Kalpasūtra*, 1.9

5 Kane, P.V., *History of Dharma Śāstras*, II, pt. 2, pp. 942-46.

elephant, tiger, buffalo and rhinoceros. A deer is carved under the seat. Sir John Marshal recognized in the motif three significant aspects of Paśupati Śiva.[1] Śiva is known in the Hindu literature as Mahāyogin, Paśupati and *Trayambaka* or three faced. As such he traces the origin of Śiva in its Paśupati form to the Indus valley. In addition to the typical yogic posture of Padmāsana drooping eyes and Penis-erectus noticed in the Mohenjodaro seals, S. R. Rao[2] has pointed out to a new evidence. He has illustrated a number of terracotta human figurines from Lothal and other Harappan sites showing a variety of yogic practices. The above evidence suggests in all probability the prevalence of yogic or ascetic practices in the Indus civilization in the 2nd and 3rd millennium B.C. in India. We do not precisely know what were the ends which the Indus people wanted to achieve through such yogic practices. On analogy from the Vedic, Epic and Classical Sanskrit literature we might infer that these practices were undertaken with a view to cultivate self control and attain supernatural powers. The above evidence also suggest that the Indus culture was to different from Vedic culture that believed in spiritual entity as Ātman. They, believed in life after death as is evident from the grave goods deposited in the burials.

It may also be inferred that the Indus people practised Vedic rituals of fire. Several fire places

---

1 Marshall, *Mohanjodaro and Indus Valley Civilisation*, I, pp. 77-78.

2 Rao, S.R. (1973), *Lothal and Indus Civiligations,* Bombay, pp. 135-143.

sometimes associated with charred animal bones and other objects have been reported from Kalibangan, Lothal[1] and other sites. Not all of these fire-pits could be religious in purpose. These evidences indicated an evidence of fire rituals, which proves both the cultures - Indus and Vedic to be the same.

V

The above account suggests atleast two elements synthesisting into the concept of the hermitages. The first element comprises of the study of the Veda and the performance of the Vedic ritual and hence marks the continuity of the Vedic tradition. The second stage is marked by the growth of spiritualism i.e. the emergence of the concept of *Ātman*, rebirth, *Karma* and *Mokṣa* perhaps by the Upanisadic age which transformed the ideological goals of the Brahmanical society. It is this new goal of spiritualism which came to be the corner stone of the life and culture of the hermitages in the epics and the *Upaniṣ ads.*

Thus the culture of the hermitages in course of time came to assimilate and synthesise the *Pravṛtti* and *Nivṛtti* paths. The limitations of the path of *Tapa* or asceticism aimed at the cultivation of will power or supernatural powers and of the Vedic study and the performance of the Vedic rituals were brought home by the lower goal of

---

1 *Ibid.*

Pravṛtti advocated by them. The *Īśāvasyopaniṣad* calls this knowledge as *Avidyā* (ignorance) and describes this as leading to dark worlds if pursued along.[1] The *Kaṭha Upaniṣad* calls their goal as *Preyas* (pleasant) as distinct from Śreyasa.[2] The newly acquired goal of spiritualism was openly declared as *vidyā* (higher knowledge) and *Śreyas*, but not in isolation of the other. What they emphasize is the synthesis of the two. The lower knowledge according to *Īśāvasyopaniṣad* is necessary for the world of existence, while the higher knowledge will lead to *Amṛtam* (immortality)[3].

The Vedic tradition was not rejected by the sages of the

Upaniṣads. On the contrary, the hermitages included the study of the Veda and the six *Vedāṅgas* in the educational curriculum. The teaching of the Veda had started as early as the Ṛgvedic times as is evident from the *Maṇḍūka Sūkta.* The *Ṛṣis* were the central figures of the Vedic schools. With the growing importance of *Mantra* and the *Yajña*, they developed an elaborate scheme of courses called the *Vedāṅga* in the later-Vedic age. The ascetic practices or Tapa even among the Ṛgvedic Ṛṣis were known. The *Tapa* continued to be emphasized in the later Vedic age too. But their goal got transformed. Instead of aiming at the cultivation of supernatural power, the hermits undertook

---

1 Īśāvasyopaniṣad, I.9.
2 Kāṭhopaniṣad, I.1.1
3 Īśa.up. I.2.

Tapa to cultivate self control as a means to the attainment of Self Realization, the summum bonum of life. By the epic age the hermitages came to be well established not only as centres for self realization but also as institutions for religious and secular education. Yet, most of the hermitages had the dominant role of Self realization (see Chapter III for details).

We have seen three main strands in the culture of the hermitages which came to be mingled and synthesized by the Upanisadic times. The socio-historic background which led to the growth of these strains and this synthesis is necessary to explain this phenomenon. It is well known that there existed a developed urban civilization in India during Vedic period. This civilization was distinguished by efficient agriculture depending on plough technology, specialization in arts and crafts and long distance trade. The society was stratified and perhaps the institution of a centralized state had come into existence.[1]

The idea of a pantheon of deities and divinities can perhaps be inferred from the depiction of human and animal figures on the seals, terra cotta mother goddesses and bulls, steatite human heads and figures etc. The sacrificial pits from Lothal[2], Kalibanga[3] etc. suggest the significance of

---

1 Suraj Bhan, (1979), Proto historic Archaeology of Sonasvati Basin (Haryana).

2 Rao, S.R., op.cit., pp. 135-143.

3 Lal, B.B. and Thapar, B.K. (1967), Excavation at Kalibanyan : New light on the Indus civilization, Cultural Forum 9(4), pp. 78-88.

rituals perhaps in the propitiation of gods. Yet the yogic postures depicted on seals from Mohen Jodaro[1] and the human figurines of clay from Lothal etc.[2] perhaps suggest the idea of acquisition of divine power or self control. These ideological concepts in addition to beliefs in animism, seem to be the varied beliefs of the complex Vedic Harappan society. The rituals and burials perhaps revealed the beliefs of the well to do sections of the society. The occurrence of fire pits suggesting Sranta Yajña and other rituals were located on a huge platform of mud-bricks within the citadel area of Kalibanga.[3] Animism seems to be practised by more primitive sections of society. But ascetic and yogic practices for obtaining divine power would be popular among those who were no more satisfied with the divine favours supposed to be obtained through rituals. They perhaps wanted to practise a life of righteousness and *tapa* in order to obtain the divine power themselves.

The Vedic literature is unique in throwing light on the growth of religious ideas in the Vedic society. The early Vedic society[4] was based on agriculture and pastoralism. A simple division of labour and the use of copper technology existed. The society was organized into *Janas* or clans and lived in *gramas* or villages and puras, cities as well. The king was elected by the and council.

---

1 Marshall, op.cit., pp. 77-78.
2 Rao, S.R., op.cit., pp. 135-143.
3 Lal, B.B. and Thapar, B.K., (1967), op.cit., pp. 78-88.
4 Sharma R.S. (1966), Light on the Early Indian Society and Economy, Bombay, pp. 52-89.

The outlook of the Ṛgvedic people was positive, spiritual worldly. They wanted to live in the world for a long period of hundred years to achieve the goal of life. The early Vedic people were immune of religious beliefs. The gods (natural powers) were acknowledged as benevolent, and responsible for the creation and maintenance of the universe. They believed that natural phenomena can be modified with the help of Yajñas to yield desired results.

In the age of *Brāhmaṇas* the Vedic society was no different from Vedic period. Vedic mysteries were explained through allegorical rituals various rituals were developed as scientific teachniques to yield rain and woudoff the same.

By the Upanisadic age, the concept of same *Jīva Ātman* in all made the situation more intolerable. The idea of *mukti* (liberation) from *Sansāra* or bondage perhaps reflects the spiritual tendency of the society and the aspirations of the masses as conceived by the thinkers of the age. The primitive goals of worldly life of the *Ṛgveda* could not satisfy the more advanced age. The idea of immortality as known in the *Brāhmaṇas* was red with the moral principle exhaustibility of the *Karmas* Premium was laid on ture knowledge, the knowledge of the nature of Self and the universe was thought to be identical. It is the identity of the individual self with the universal self which forms the fundamental teachings of *Upaniṣads*.

The ascetic strain of the pre-Vedic age continued to survive in the Vedic age also as known from the *Keśin Sūkta* and references to *Muni* etc. the idea seems to have been evolved or adapted by the vedic people in their own conditions. While the Vedic rituals and prayers aimed at yielding natural favour for material gains, asceticism or Yoga was supposed to bestow the divine power itself. The major revolution in their ideology, however, came with the concept of Ātman associated with the idea of rebirth, *Karma* and *Mukti*. Hence, it seems that the various strands which went into the making of the culture of the hermitages represent only the different shades of stages in the growth of idealistic thought in the socio-historical condition of Indian society.

VI

The further transformation of the hermitages into centres of eclectic education or universities was the next important stage in the history of the hermitages. Perhaps the educational institutions had come to be established in or near the cities and towns.

Educatuional practice was well developed from Vedic times.

The transformation of the hermitages or *viharas* into educational institutions or universities seems to be the product of advanced urban life in the early history. The *Jātaka* accounts tell us about the pupils coming from distant places like Mithilā, Rājagṛha, Ujjayinī, Śivi and Kuru Kingdoms to Takṣaśilā (Taxila in Pakistan) for receiving education under world renowned teachers. The *Jātakas* also mentions *Vāraṇasī* or Benaras as a great seat at Takṣaśila[1]. The city of Ayodhyā is also said to have the schools of Vedic and Purānic learning. With the growth of Buddhism and Jainism the institution of Vihāra emerged but it followed the traditional pattern of the hermitages. Though Buddha organized the *Saṅgha* more scientifically and on democratic basis following the pattern prevailing among the tribal states in those days. In course of time these *Vihāras* became important centres of learning.

Mithilā or Videh had become a prominent seat of Brahmanical learning by the Upaniṣadic age. Janaka used to hold religious conferences and philosophical discussions where scholars like Yājñavalkya were invited[2].

Takṣaśilā was one of the most important centers which came into being about the time of the Buddha if not earlier. It had a widespread reputation in and outside India and attracted hundreds of scholars from various parts of the world. But it had already been deserted by the 5th century A.D. when Fa-hian visited India. In the time of Alexander it was famous for its philosophers and scholars. The curriculum of higher education at this centre included the study of the *Vedas*, *Vedāṅgas* and the Buddhist literature.

---

1 Jataka, No. 252, 11-82.

2 Rai, B.C. History of Indian Education, Lucknow, pp. 74-75.

The scientific or technical subjects such as *Ayurveda*, Surgery, *Dhanurvidyā*, Jyotiṣa, trade and commerce, music, dancing and painting etc. were also taught at Taxila in addition to the Greek languages, architecture and arts. The place continued to remain a centre of learning upto 455 A.D.[1].

Kāśī also emerged as an important source of Aryan culture and education. It came to be manned by Acharyas from Takṣaśilā. In the early historic phase of urbanization pupils flocked at Benaras from distant parts for studies in various branches of knowledge including the Vedic studies and the eighteen crafts[2].

The ancient ruins of Nālanda lie seven miles to the north of Rajgriha and 40 miles in the south east of Patna. It was associated with Buddha and Mahavīra in Indian tradition. But the university seems to have come into existence in the 3rd century A.D. or so. Nāgārjuna, the famous Buddhist scholar and Āryadeva were associated with this university. Fa-hian visited Nālandā in 410 A.D. At this time of Hieun-Tsang, there lived 1510 teachers at Nālandā. It attracted scholars not only from India, but also

---

1 Ibid. pp. 2-65; Das, S.K. (1930) The Educational System of Ancient Hindus, Calcutta, pp. 307-14; Altaker, A.S., (1957), Education in Ancient India, Varanasi, pp. 106-112; Mitraveda (1967), Education in Ancient India, New Delhi, pp. 107-109; Sharan, B., (1969), Gurukula Systems of Education and Its application to Modern times, Varanasi, pp. 177-84.

2 Rai, B.C., op.cit., pp. 65-67; Altekar, A.S., (1957), op.cit., pp. 112-116; Das, S.K. (1930), op.cit., pp. 385-86.

from China, Korea, Java etc. Although it was a *Mahāyāna Vihāra*, but there existed arrangements for the teaching of *Hinayāna* scriptures, the Veda, *Vedāṅgas, Sāṅkhya, Dharma Śāstras, Purāṇas, Jyotiṣa, Ayurveda* etc. The university was destroyed at the end of the 12th century by Bakhtiar Khilji[1].

Besides these universities grew at Valabhi[2] in Gujrat, Oadantapuri[3] and Vikramaśila[4] in the Gangetic valley, Jagaddala[5], Ranchi[6] and Nadia[7] etc. in the south.

The hermitages went out of fashion or were replaced by *Viharas* and educational institutions after the Gupta age. The temples also became the centres of gravity in the society. The students went to the temple to learn, the household went to worhship, while the ascetics established there *maṭhas.* The tradition of hermitages got transformed into *viharas* and *maṭhas.* Renunciation became mental rather than a physical activity and the *Aśramas* or the four stages of life come to be replaced by four stages of *Bhakti.* It is interesting that the later (*Smṛtis* like those of *Nārada*

---

1 Rai, B.C., op.cit., pp. 67-71; Sankalia, H.D., University of Nalanda; Sharma, B. (1968) op.cit., pp. 184-194.

2 Rai, B.C., op.cit., pp. 71-72; Altekar, A.B., op.cit., 125-127; Sankalia, H.D., op.cit., pp. 179 ff.

3 Rai, B.C., op.cit., p. 73; Sankalia, H.D., op.cit., p. 189.

4 Rai, B.C., op.cit., pp. 72-73; Altekar, A.S. (1957), op.cit., pp. 127-131.

5 Rai, B.C., op.cit., pp. 73-74.

6 *Ibid.,* p.76.

7 See Nadia Gayetteer (Bengal District Gagetteer No. 24) 1910, p. 180; See also Adam's Reports, p.49; Rai, B.C., ibid., p.75.

(500 A.D.) and *Bṛhaspati* (600 A.D.) did not contain chapter on *Aśramas* unlike the earlier *Sūtras* and *Smṛtis.* The reason for this transformation of the institution of the hermitage perhaps corresponds with the socio-economic changes in the society. The growth of urbanisation and the patronage by the ruling classes to the educational institutions helped in their transformation into the universities. Besides, this was the age of scholastic thinking which followed the spontaneous thinking of the age of the Upaniṣads and the Buddha. The emphasis was laid now on cultivation of reason and provide rationale to the philosophical thinking of the earlier ages. The growth of complexity in the society put forward more demands of qualified or skilled men in different areas of social activity. With the growth of technology and surplus accumulation the society could now afford to organize and maintain the educational and religious institutions to serve the needs of the society better.

CHAPTER-5

THE ROLE OF THE HERMITAGES

A critical study of the hermitages shows that there was uniform nature of these institutions in Ancient India. The scope of their activities was almost same slightly varying from hermitage to hermitage and from age to age as per requirements of time and place. In fact, the pattern for the hermitage was set by the patriarch sage. The chief function of the hermitages seems to be the fulfillment of the spiritual and material goal as conceived by the society of the age. By the time of the later Vedic or the Epic age which marks the fullfledged growth of the hermitages, the Vedic society had become complex. It witnessed the development of territorial states and the march towards urbanisation. The institution of the hermitage seems to be product of these conditions and aimed at seeking answer to the problems facing the society of the age.

It has already been seen that the functions of the hermitages generally included the cultivation of spiritual powers and self control through ascetic practices and the realization of the Self. But the chief goal that dominated the culture of the hermitages and the Upanisadic age had been identified with the search for identity in Ātman. The hermitages also served the purpose of training the people in specialized arts and crafts prevalent at that time. Although educational training in the skill of the arms, arts and crafts was given only in a limited number of hermitages. The teaching of Veda and *Vedāṅgas* and the performance of Vedic rituals was, however, a common feature though not the chief objective before the hermits. The persons who came to the forest were not the raw youth or the aged alone, they generally represented men and women full of physical, intellectual and moral spirit. They represented one of the very sensitive elements of the society seeking the solution of the problem of suffering in the world[1].

I

The chief outcome of this search for the solution of the problem of pain and suffering in the world was the growth of idealistic thought showing different stages of growth and varied forms of its manifestation. One of the earlier objectives seems to be the acquisition of spiritual powers through ascetic practices. But the major break-through in the perspective of the life of hermits came with the discovery of the concept of Ātman as the Ultimate Reality permeating the universe and transcending it as an eternal, all pervading, omniscient and omnipotent entity. It was conceived as distinct from the material world which was changeful and unconscious and dependent on the Ātman. The careful observation, hermits to perceive the nature of Ātman as Synonymous with *Satyam-Jñānam-Anantam* as described in the *Upaniṣads*. A comparison with the four states of man – *Jagrat, Svapan, Nidrā* and *Turīya* –

---

1 Chenchiah, P. et.al., *Aśramas - Past and Present,* Madras, p. 104.

perhaps brought home to the sages the nature of Ātman as blissful, psychological and eternal. The suffering was explained as resulting from ignorance of the Reality and the consequent hankering after the endless wants and desires of worldly pleasure which were not permanent assets. The resultant *Karma* according to them led to rebirth and suffering.

Naturally, this line of thinking brought home the need for removing the cause of suffering through the realization of Ātman and not being duped by the attraction of the transitory pleasures of the world. Hence, the forests were thought to be a suitable place for the realization of the goal, away as they were from the hum-drum of the worldly life and perhaps for the sanctity attached to them in primitive thought. The goal formulated in the light of the above aimed at self Realization which was supposed to lead to the cessation of the cycle of birth and death and to the identity of individual Self (Jivātman) with the universal Self (Brahman).

Radhakrishnan points out when he says that, 'The ideal man of India is not the magnanimous man of Greece or the valiant knight of medieval Europe, but the free man of spirit who has attained insight into the universal source by rigid discipline and practice of disinterested virtues, who had freed himself from the prejudices of time and place. It is India's pride that she has clung fast to this ideal and produced in every generation and in every part of the country...... men who strove successfully to realize this ideal'.[1]

The growth of the idealistic thought the chief teaching of the *Upaniṣads* and the Epic literature provided a new sense of identity and helped forging unity in diversity, the central theme of Indian culture. It provided new hope for the future in a world of sorrows and miseries and led to the transformation of their world outlook and social institutions.

The cyclic concepts of the transmigration of soul and the theory of *Manvantara* together with the doctrine of *Karma* explained the problem of birth and death of individual and the origin and end of the universe. The social stratification and the disabilities were provided rationale by the concepts towards the society and, the entire living world, intergrated through the concept of *Ātman.*

The influence of idealistic thought in promoting a sense of identity between man and man and even with lower creatures helped the growth of more profound perception of morality. The response resulted in the recognition of one's duty to other human beings and other living creatures in a social environment of competing interests saturated with selfishness. The values like contentment, tolerance, humility, austerity, chastity and truthfulness marked the life of the hermits. This value system was consciously

---

1 Quoted by Sharma, D.S., *What is Hinduism,* p.66.

cultivated by the pupils in the hermitages under the disciplined and enlightened guidance of the hermits.

II

The hermitages seem to have played a significant role in the process of acculturation of the tribes and people in the country. India is known for the diversity of people and geographical background. The humanistic thought of the hermitages helped in bringing unity among people with varied cultural and ethnic backgrounds. The concept of *Ātman* created a sense of identity, generated faith and confidence among each other which facilitated interaction and co-operation. The location of the hermitages in the forests inhabited by the tribal people hastened the pace of acculturation and the spread of the synthetic Indian culture. These hermits virtually served as missionaries of the Indian culture and helped the tribal people emerged out of their barbaric beliefs and pattern of life.

The impact of the culture of the hermitages was felt on the society of the civilized world also. It helped in raising the general tone of individual and social morality by subducing ego, arrogance, hypocracy and selfishness. It taught them to be more sensitive and responsive to the suffering of humanlord and thus helped in mitigating the harshness and cruelities in relations with men and animals. Naturally, *Ahiṁsā* came to the corner stone of Indian culture. Significance of the role of hermitages has been well brought out by Radha Krishnan who opines that,"Spiritual life is the true genius of hermitages in India. Those who make the greatest appeal to the Indian mind are not the military conquerors, nor the rich merchants or the great diplomats but the holy sages or seers who embody spirituality at its best and purest. India has produced these holy men in every generation and in every part of the country from the time of her recorded history who possessed all that the country held most dear and sacred. Though they generally remained away from the main stream of life, kings and commoners pay reverent homage to them and take their advice in the problem of their personal lives as well as public affair. By their lives they teach us that pride and power, wealth and glory are nothing in comparison with the power of spirit. It is those who scorn their own lives that raise our life above all scorns[1].

III

The hermitages did not exist in isolation. The hermits were away from the social needs. They studied their environment in detail and this opportunity for close observation and analysis was provided to them by their close association with the forests. As such, they discovered the properties of various herbs and their utility to man and other creatures. They also examined the behavior of animals around them. This led to the growth of the

---

1 Introduced by S. Radha Krishnan (1958), *The Cultural Heritage of India*, IED, Calcuta, p. XXIII.

rudiments of the sciences of Medicine, Botany and Zoology. Astronomy and music were also cultivated in the hermitages[1].

But what happened to be the major contribution in the field of sciences was Yoga and human psychology. Aurobindo hints at it when he raises the question,"What was the secret of that gigantic intellectuality, spirituality and superhuman moral force which we see in the *Rāmāyaṇa* and *Mahābhārata*, ancient philosophy, in classical Sanskrit literature, in the supereme poetry, art, sculpture and architecture of India. It would be an error to look for the secret of Aryan success in the details of the instruction given in the old hermitages and universities so far as they have come down to us. We shall find the secret of their success in a profound knowledge of human psychology and its subtle application to the methods of intellectual training and instructions."[2]

IV

The hermitages led to the growth of vast literature required to be used by the pupils as well as by the society. The *Āraṇyakas* and the *Upaniṣads* were unmistakably the product of the culture of hermitages. It is not unlikely that many a hymn to the Vedic seers were revealed in the forest dwellings. Besides, the study of the Veda and the

---

1 Chenchiah, P. et.al., op.cit., p. 109.
2 Sri Aurobindo, (1948), The Brain of India, IV Ed., pp. 11-12.

performance of rituals formed part of the educational curriculum of the hermitages. The emphasis on the knowledge of Veda and Vedic rituals pointed to the utilitarian aspects of it. This helped the pupils as well as the hermits to eke out their livelihood in the society. The rituals and the Vedic studies in the hermitages of course represented the Vedic tradition of the society.

Their continued importance led to the growth of the Vedic sciences – the six Vedāṅgas i.e. Sikṣā (the science of phonetics), Kalpa (the science of figurative rituals), Vyakarana (Grammar), Nirukta (Philology), Chhandas (Prosody) and Jyotisha (Astronomy)?

Apart from the growth of Vedic literature there also grew Epic and Puranic literature under the influence of the hermitages.

The *Rāmāyaṇa*, the *Mahābhārata* and the *Purāṇas* respresent the synthesis of the Vedic culture with that of the hermitages. The message was passed through legends and stories to cultivate the new value systems among the illiterate masses. A similar synthetic approach is also traced in the *Dharmaśāstras*. This helped in the transformation of the Vedic culture into a universal culture or the transformation of the *Vedic-dharma* into the *Mānava-dharma*[1].

---

1 Altekar, A.S. (1957), *Eucation in Ancient India*, Varanasi, p. 328.

The ancient *Ṛṣis* and sages of the forest were great lovers of nature as well. There are many hymns and poems which can be regarded as descriptions of the beautiful and sublime aspects of nature. Bahadurmal emphasizes that, "The bright expanse of heaven, the broad sunlit earth with its green meadows, the luxurious vegetation and flowing rivers, the glorious sun, the beautiful dawn preceding sun-rise, the life-giving waters, the cool breezes, the refreshing showers of rain, the bright fire, the dark mysterious night and incessantly flowing rivers made a deep impression in the minds of these poet-philosophers and gave rise to a highly powerful poetry which can be compared with the best of its kind in the world."[1]

The knowledge thus cultivated in the hermitages was disseminated in the society through their pupils and social contacts. The in depth study of a variety of disciplines ultimately provided the basis for the growth of educational and training institutions and services in the society. The ambition to excel in intellectual sphere resulted in open discussions and debates among scholars and philosophers which helped the dissemination of knowledge in the society at large.

The hermitages naturally came to be the temples of learning and self culture. They played a vital role in the cultivation and diffusion of Indian culture. Rabindra Nath Tagore points out that, "A most wonderful thing we notice

---

1 Bahadurmal, (1956), *Indian Culture,* Hashiarpur, pp. 104-111.

in India is that here the forest, not the town, is the fountainhead of all its civilization. Wherever in India its earliest and most wonderful manifestation are noticed we find that men have not come into such close contact as to be rolled or fused into a compact mass. There, trees and plants, rivers and lakes had an ample opportunity to live in close relationship with humans. In these forests though there was human society, there was enough of open space of aloofeness, there was no jostling. Still this aloofness, did not produce inertia in the Indian mind, rather it rendered it all the brighter. It is the forest that has nurtured the two great ancient ages of India, the Vedic and the Buddhist. As did the Vedic Ṛṣis, Lord Buddha also showered his teaching in the many woods of India. The current of civilization that flowed from its forests inundated the whole of India".[1]

V

The contribution of the hermitages was unimaginably great. The institution not only grew as an attempt to solve the problem of pain and suffering. But it worked out real solution to the problem by analyzing its causes scientifically. It came out with a real remedy of all human problems giving rise to highly advance science and technology and eliminated abhāva (poverty) and suffering. They also helped develop a real perception towards the

---

1 Quoted by Mukherji, R.K. (1969), *Ancient Indian Education*, Delhi, p. XXXV.

realities of life. The realization of Self was suggested as the main goal of life. Their attempt was also at rationalisation of the real conditions of life. Rationalisation is a natural human tendency to minimize the importance of material things which are not so important in life as considered to be. The wants and desires were verified as the product of ignorance. This meant the liberation from all material belongings of life. The change of attitude towards life brings a real transformation. It created an attitude of indifference and lack of concern for the worldly things which are not so material. This promoted a balanced growth of science and technology at physical and metaphysical level and the actual scientific understanding of human and his environment.

This minimized the probability of struggle among human beings and survival of all was ensured instead of the survival of fittest. The growth of idealistic thought generated humanism, promoted moral and ethical values that helped the transformation of society in the real sense. It generated a hope of future redemption. It explained away the sufferings as the consequence of one's own past actions and urged the people to understand their duties towords society, nation and environment. In short it promoted spiritualism and completely discarded the upswing of an unjust social system. It taught one's individual welfare is co-terminus with the welfare of entire society. This promoted the growth of positive attitude in life and virtually posed no major danger to the social system. In the last analysis, therefore, the growth of hermitages strengthened the fabric of life by providing a real vision to words life and helped the assuage of suffering permantely.

CHAPTER – VI

CONCLUSION

The present study has thrown light on several important aspects of the institution of hermitages in ancient India particularly on their life and culture, origin and development and contribution to society. The study which mainly concentrated on the Brāhmanical and classical Sanskrit literature has brought to our notice 75 hermitages.[1] The bulk of these hermitages occur in the great epics, *Rāmāyaṇa* containing an account of 24 hermitages and the *Mahābhārata* recording 34 of them with only the hermitages of Agastya and Vasiṣṭha being common to the two works.

I

The geographical description of the hermitages shows their distribution in the Sarasvati-Ganga plains, the Himalayan and the Vindhyan hills[2]. The *Rāmāyaṇa* reveals their association with the central Gangetic Valley and the Vindhyan regions. But the hermitages of the *Mahābhārata* point to their location in the Madhya deśa. The more or less exclusive but contiguous distribution of the hermitages in the two epics perhaps suggests the contemporary existence of the hermit-culture zones or the distinct spheres of influence of the two epics. The Buddhist literature also refer to 3 hermitages[3]. None of these is, however, found

---

1 Vide *supra* chapter II, and infra. Appendex II.

2 Vide *infra* Appendix III.

mentioned in the epics. The early *Purāṇas* contained an account of 11 hermitages only.[1] Of these 5 occur in the *Mahābhārata*, while the remaining 6 are new and have not been mentioned in any of the earlier works. The Classical Sanskrit literature also records a few of the hermitages. Kalidāsa refers to 4 hermitages, all of which are mentioned in the epics.[2] The later Sanskrit literature mentioned 8 new hermitages[3]. This shows that most of the hermitages belonged to the epic age and only a few came into being in the later age of the Classical Sanaskrit literature.

The hermitages were traditionally associated with the forests. The *Daṇḍaka, Janmasthāna, Dvaitavana, Kāmyaka* and the *Naimiṣa* forests were their popular resorts[4]. The hermitages lay both in the plains as well as in the hills generally on river sides. The important rivers associated with the hermitages included the Ganges, Tamasā, Sarayū, Narmadā, Mandākīni, Sarasvati, Apagā, Gomatī, Sadānirā, etc.[5] A few of the hermitages have also been mentioned on lake sides.[6]

The important hills inhabited by the hermits included the Himalayas, Vindhyas, *Citrakūṭa, Ṛsyamuka, Vaidūrya Parvata* and the *Sumeru.*[7] Only a few of the

---

3 Vide *infra* Appendix II.
1 Vide *infra*, Appendix II.
2 Vide *infra*, Appendix II.
3 Ibid.
4 Vide *infra*, Appendix III.
5 Ibid.
6 Ibid.

hermitages were associated with the towns.[1] The most important of such hermitages were those of Sandīpani at Avanti, of Bhairavāchārya near Thanesar, that of Jahnu perhaps at Sultanganj[2], and of Kukkuṭarāma at Pataliputra[3] etc. It is interesting that all of these hermitages are found mentioned in very late Sanskrit works. In the earlier period or the epic age the hermits generally preferred forests or isolated places away from the hum-drum of the towns. But there seems to be a special liking for a picturesque landscape full of trees, plants and wild animals providing the varied natural environment. The supply of water, wild fruits and roots seem to be the major consideration for locating the hermitages.

II

The subsistence of the inmates of the hermitages depended generally on the products of the jungle, collection of grains, begging of alms, gifts from the royal personages and the rich, fees from the pupils and cattle keeping. The pupils had the responsibility of tending the cattle and collecting roots and fruits, firewood and the alms. The kings and princes visited the hermitages when they were out for hunting or when they wanted to invoke the grace of god through the good offices of the holy sages for the birth of a male child. Hospitality was a conspicuous feature of the

---

7 Ibid.
1 Ibid.
2 Law, B.C. (1976), op.cit., p.223.
3 Sharma, J.S. (1972), op.cit., p. 106.

culture of the hermits. They treated the guests extremely honourably, *arghya*, washed their hands and feet, offered them the best available food and provided them place for rest. The hermitages generally included several huts, some of which contained more than one chambers. Separate places were set apart in the hermitages for the daily rituals or *Agnihotra* and the worship of the gods. The hermits lived with their families and pupils leading a life of austerity and penances. The household equipment of the hermitages was extremely simple. Their dress comprised of bark of the trees and their huts were made of daub grass and leaves. The sacrificial utensils, waterpots, clothes and the cows were their only assets. Their life was disciplined and hard. They lived mainly on fruits, roots, grains and the cow's milk. They ate only twice a day and observed fasts frequently.

The daily routine of the hermitages included the performance of spiritual rites, penances, meditation and Svādhāya or the study of the Veda and the subjects related to spirituality, philosophy and the *Vedāṅgas*.[1] The hermits maintained regularity in the study of the Veda. They led a life of austerity and self mortification to achieve control over senses. Some of the hermits practiced *Pañchāgni* penance by sitting between fires on all the four sides in the scorching sunlight, some others lived on raw food, some

---

[1] Vide *supra*, chapter III.

did not avail of any rest, some lived in the open, some wore wet clothes, while some lived on waters as is known from the description of the hermitages of Janasthāna in the *Rāmāyaṇa.*[1]

The hermitages also served as educational hubs of the epic age. The pupils lived with the hermits as members of their family. The sages were highly respected in the society. The students' life was characterized by simplicity, austerity, hard work, discipline and celibacy. The teaching was both verbal and written and imparted only to the deserving candidates. The educational curriculum included the study of the *Veda* and the *Vedāṅgas.*[2] Some of the harmitages were famous centres for the study of science of arms. The hermitages of Droṇa and Gotama Sāradavat are well known for the teaching of the skill in arms.[3] The *Rāmāyaṇa* refers to several classes of teachers. But it was still a secondary function. They grew into whole time educational institutions[4] in the later ages. We know about the growth of university like Taxila, Nālandā etc. Their eclectic atmosphere was praiseworthy. Bāṇa refers to the hermitage of Divākarāmitra where pupils subscribing to radically different doctrines and sects lived together for obtaining knowledge. Among these students were included

---

1 Vide *supra*, chapter II.
2 Ibid.
3 Vide *infra*, Appendix IV.
4 Vide *supra*, Appendix IV.

the digambaras, Svetāmbaras, Bhāgavatas, Saṁkhyas, Lokayatikas and Brāhmanical ascetics.[1]

A hermit lived with his wife who assisted him in the performance of his duties. Some of the ladies themselves took to the vows of hermits. The *Rāmāyaṇa* refers to women hermits like Ansuyā, Śavarī[2] etc. The fact that Śavarī, a tribal woman, could become a hermit, it appears that the membership of the hermitages was open to all, without any distinction of male or female, caste or creed.

III

The earliest mention of *Aśramas* or *Tapovanas* is found in the *Rāmāyaṇa* and the *Mahābhārata* where these terms have been clearly used in the sense of an abode of ascetics, *Vānaprasthas* or *Bhikṣus*. These forest resorts, the abode of hermits, their wives, children and disciples, were meant for undergoing *Tapa* (penances), self control and cultivating the knowledge of the self. Their orthodox character was indicated by the study of the Veda and the performance of the simple Vedic ritual (*Agnihotra*). Although the main objective of the hermits was religious and esoteric, the hermitages for all practical purposes served as the educational institutions for cultivating the knowledge of the *Veda* and the *Vedāṅgas*.

---

1 *Bāṇa Harṣācarit,* Cowell and Thomas (Eng. Tr.) pp. 236-37.

2 Sinha Jadunath (1956), *A History of Indian Philosophy,* Culcutta, pp. 4-41.

There is no direct reference to the hermitages in the Vedic literature Vadas, however, mentions *puras*, meaning towns and cities. But *Āraṇyakas* and *Upaniṣads* were unmistakably the products of the forest dwelling hermits, ascetics or sages. Vedic literature emphasized study, intellectual reflection and meditation as the means to intellectual conviction about the nature of Ātman. Discipline of body and mind and practice of Yoga purify mind and make it fit to acquire knowledge of Ātman. *Bṛhadāraṇyaka Upaniṣad* considers *Śama, dama, Uparati, Titikṣā* and *Samādhi* as pre-requisites for the realization of *Ātman*, the summum bonnum of life[1]. The *Upaniṣads* refer to *Vidyā* and *Avidyā* and *Parāvidyā* and *Aparā-Vidyā* to distinguish higher knowledge (of *Ātman*) from the lower knowledge (of worldly goals).

Correspondingly, they talk of *Śreyas* (the ultimate good) and the *Preyas* (the pleasant) ends. Neither of these were exclusively thought to be conducive to the attainment of the real goal. They emphasized a balance of the two as the right course[2]. Although the *Upaniṣads* reveal unified philosophy, Vedānta seems to be the culminating theme of these works[3]. The knowledge of *Ātman* or Brahman was viewed as *Guhiyam* (secret) or *Rahasyam* (esoteric) and was to be taught in secret sessions to the deserving pupils[4].

---

1 Vide *supra*, chapter IV.
2 Sinha Jadunath (1956), op.cit.
3 Vide *supra*, Chapter IV.
4 Vide *infra*, Appendix V.

It is evident from the above that the culture of the *Āraṇyakas* and *Upaniṣads* more or less breathe the atmosphere of spiritualism and asceticism as the epics do. The *Āraṇyakas* and *Upaniṣads* refer to *Śrāmaṇas, Tāpasas* and *Vaikhānasas.* Besides, certain nemes of the epic hermits, namely, Bhāradvāja, Bhārgava, Viśvāmitra, Jamadagni etc. also occur in the *Āraṇyakas* and the *Upaniṣads*[1]. Thus, the existence of hermitages could be inferred from the internal evidence of these works in this age which does not seem to be far removed from the epic age.

Even though the *Saṁhitās* and the *Brāhmaṇas* do not contain direct account of the hermitages, there is ample evidence to suggest the prevalence of asceticism in the Vedic age. The references to *Yatis, Munis* and *Brahmacharins* in the *Ṛgveda*, later *Saṁhitās* and the *Brāhmaṇas* hint at the existence of ascetics and asceticism in the pre-Upanisadic age[2]. The *Yatis*, who were associated with the Bhṛgus perhaps represented a class of ascetics exercising self control. Keśin hymn is devoted to a class of ascetics having long hair and identical with fire, wind and sun and performing *Tapa*. The Munis have been described as having long hair moving in the sky at will, dwelling in both the oceans, following the path of beasts (in the forest) and upholding fire, moisture, heaven and earth. In the

---

1 Vide *supra*, Chapter IV.
2 Ibid.

Atharvaveda, the muni is stated to be the master of spiritual powers obtained through penance. He is referred as wearing yellow and soiled cloth and moving along the wind and obtaining of divine status. The term *Vrātya* also means an ascetic practicing *Tapa* and having divine powers. They were respected by intellectuals as well as the kings[1]. The term like *Yatis* and *Brahmacharins* also occur in other later Vedic literature. Besides, the names of several Ṛgvedic *Ṛsis* happen to be associated with the hermitages in the epics[2].

But the *Ṛgveda* has predominently wordly outlook. The *Ṛgvedic* people wanted to live life for hundred years. They asked for heroic sons and riches. The gods, supposed to be powerful beings representing the various phenomena of nature, were propitiated through prayers and sacrifices to fulfill their desire. This shows a positive attitude to life in the *Ṛgveda* as against the other-worldly attitude of the hermitage culture.

Whether the ascetic tradition noticed above was indigenous to the Ṛgvedic culture or it had a different source has been a subject of great controversy. H.D. Sharma has suggested Vedic origin of the ascetic tradition[3]. He thinks that the *Pravṛtti* and *Nivṛtti*, both originated in the same Vedic tradition as is evident from the internal

---

1 Vide *infra*, Appendix V.
2 Sharma, H.D. (1939), op.cit.
3 Vide *supra*, Chapt. IV.

evidence of the *Ṛgveda* described above. His contention is also supported by the occurrence of monasticism in the Greek culture[1]. He invokes the evidence of Uttarājjhan, a Jain text, showing how the sensitive minds reacted to the brutalities of human execution and animal sacrifice[2]. Scholars like G.C. Pandey, R.C. Chandra, Sukumar Dutt and others, on the other hand, have suggested that the religious mendicancy was non-Vedic and pre-Vedic in its origin[3]. They associate the Śrāmanic tradition with the pre-Vedic Indus culture[4]. But their ideas appear to be born of ignorance Śramnic tradition is very much Vedic as miggested by the entire vedic literature. In fact, Indus culture has also been proved as Vedic on by modern researches.

The antiquity of Yoga or ascetism is attested by both the Vedic Indus civilisation and Paśupati seals from Mohenjodaro, other sculptures and also from terracotta human figurines showing various Yogic poses all but point out Vedic basis of Indus civilization. The belief in the Mother goddess, male deities, animism etc. life after death and rituals, suggest all suggest the oneness of the Vedic and the Indus ages.

Both the ritualistic and the ascetic strands in their own imagination aimed at the fulfillment of man's desires

---

1 Ibid.
2 Ibid.
3 Ibid.
4 Vide *supra*, Chapt. IV.

by invoking divine powers through the recitation of sacred formulas and performance of the rituals, or by endowing oneself with spiritual or divine powers through penances and Yogic practices. Their roots perhaps lie in the primitive beliefs dominated by sympathetic magic. Perhaps the ascetic beliefs and practices happened to be manifested in varied shape in different societies from very remote times.

Whatever may be the antiquity of asceticism in India, the study of the Veda and the performance of the Vedic rituals positively relates the hermitages to the Vedic tradition. It placed before the hermits the goal of Self-realization and *Mokṣa* superceding the material gains like, wealth, children, properity. It was in this sense that the knowledge of *Ātman* was openly declared by the Vedic sages as *Parā Vidyā* or *Śreyas.* The concepts of *Ātman*, rebirth and *karma* provided a new world outlook.

It were these hermitages which seem to have provided the arch type for the Buddhist Viharas though more consciously formulated and planned to meet the changing needs of the *Bhikṣus.* The tradition of the hermitages degenerated in course of time into the *Maṭhas* of later ages. But, some of these hermitages and the *Vihāras* developed into important centres of higher learning or universities[1]. These ancient universities or *Vihāras* played a significant role in the spread of religious and secular education. The most conspicuous feature of these later

---

1 Vide *supra*, Chapt. IV.

institutions was the eclectic atmosphere where students and teachers of different religious ideologies could live and study together[1]. The important among these universities were Mithilā, Takshasilā, Kāshī, Nālandā, Jagaddāla, Kañchi, Nadia,Vikramśilā, Oadantpuri, Vallabhi etc[2].

IV

The institutions are products of social need. The hermitages too had been evolved to meet the demands of the times. These institutions aimed at the search for solution of the problem of pain and suffering in the world. The earlier solution conceived by the Ṛgvedic thinkers as also by other societies was by way of propitiation of gods through prayers and rituals. The acquisition of divine or spiritual powers through penance and ascetic practices was another approach which was adopted by the ancients in the Vedic as well as the post-Vedic ages. Both the above modes of religious life following the accomplishment of the goal of pain and suffering were superseded by spiritualism of the Upanisadic age. This marked a major change in the world outlook of the people. Their goals were transformed from *Preyas* to *Śreyas* as the *Upaniṣads* have aptly described. The material world came to be viewed as impermanent and changeful and hence of little consequence. But the immanent and transcendent psychic principle called Ātman was conceived as the Ultimate Reality, the realization of

1 Ibid.
2 Vide *supra*, Chapt. IV.

which was believed to bring about cessation of rebirth and suffering.

The vision of Vedic seers brought home the supreme need for Self realization and to reject the transitory pleasures of the world. Naturally, Self realization or *Mokṣa* came to be the chief ideal. The concept of Ātman provided a new sense of identity which was universal in character. It provided new hope for future in a world of sorrow and suffering. The doctrine of rebirth, explained away the causes by invoking innate qualities and *Karmas* of men. The *Manvantara* theory provided a cyclic explanation of the origin and dissolution of creation.

The influence of the spiritual thought came to be felt on the social institutions and goals. The concept of *Jivan-mukta* demanded the institution of *Sannyāsa* in the graduated scheme of *Aśramas.* This seems to have resulted in the synthesis of spiritual and the materialistic goals leading to the formulation of the conception of *Puruṣārtha-Catuṣṭaya* (*Dharma, Artha, Kāma, Mokṣa*), the fourfold goal of life.

With the emergence of a wider sense of identity between man and man and even with all living beings resulting from the omniscient, omnipresent and omnipotent character and immanent and transcendent nature of Ātman, a new sense of moral ethos was born. The principle of *Ahiṁsā* was consciously advocated as a code of conduct for the seekers of Ātman which, in course of time, influenced all religious sects of the country. A theory of social obligation and a fuller life was formulated resulting in the concept of three *Ṛṇas* (debts) and five *Mahāyajñas* (great Yajñas). The value system emphasizing tolerance, contentment, austerity, chastity and truthfulness marked the culture of the hermitages, and the social life could not remain uninfluenced by these humanistic values. The new sense of moral consciousness helped in tonning up the individual and social morality as a whole.

The hermitages contributed significantly to the growth of spiritual literature in ancient India.[1] The *Āraṇyakas* and the *Upaniṣadas* were unmistakably the gift of these institutions. The natural environment and the atmosphere of freedom motivated the creative impulse of the sages and helped the growth of Epic and Puranic literature. The epic and pauranic literature is permeated by the ideas and the spirit of the hermitages. The spiritual message of these institutions was passed on to the lowest stratum in the society through legends and stories which brought about sanskritisation and spiritualization of the common masses. The Vedic culture thus got transformed into a universal culture. The Vedic *dharma* became *Mānavadharma*.

The hermitages served the society also by disseminating education. The study of the *Veda* and

---

[1] Vide *supra*, Chapt. V.

Vedāṅgas and the knowledge of the Vedic rituals had its use in the society. Similarly, the study of the *Vedāṅgas* and *Upavedas* had their utilitarian aspects. In course of time these institutions and the *Viharas* emerged as reputed seats of learning.[1]

The hermitages practically served as centres of missionary activities in the diffusion of spiritual culture among the people of the country having diverse ethnic and geographical backgrounds. The humanistic idea of the hermitages and the concept of Ātman generated the necessary faith and confidence and facilated greater interaction and co-operation among different people. The location of the hermitages in the forests helped the process of acculturation and the emergence of synthetic Indian culture. On the other hand, the culture of the hermitages characterized by values of austerity, patience, tolerance, love and self-control must had its impact on the civilized world as well. It seems to have smoothed the egoistic, arrogant, hypocritic and selfish attitude of the ruling classes. It is no wonder, therefore, that the Indian society remained largely free from the slavery based social system and the brutal treatment of the slaves, conquered people and the believers of alien faiths.

Further, the hermitages promoted the growth of ancient sciences like medicine, botany, zoology, astronomy, mathematics psychology, etc.[2] The close

---

[1] Vide *supra*, Chapt. V.

association of the hermits with nature and their efforts at the control of their senses helped them in studying their natural environment and the human nature more closely. They discovered through close observation and experimentation the properties of various herbs and plants, the nature and behavior of various animals and planets and the behavior of man himself. Some of the hermitages specialized in the study of the science of the Vedas i. e. *Vedāṅgas* and the science of arms (*Dhanurveda*).[1]

The hermitages, in fact, came into existence to solve the problems of pain and suffering and provided a real solution to the problem. These institutions taught and propagated the insignificance of the material world and the realization of Self as the most cherished goal. This, in fact, amounted to more rationalization of the conditions that were full of abhāva (poverty), suffering and the fear of death. The hermitages suggested change of one's attitude towards the worldly life rather than changing the conditions of existence. This promoted an attitude of development of self with regard to nature which boosted the growth of *māntrika* science and technology alongwith the material one. The isolated existence of the hermitages away from the life of toil and exertion in the society offered real solutions and solace. The humanistic ideals fostered by the hermitages, helped in reducing the tensions, and transforming the society as a whole. The scientific *Varṇa*

---

2 Ibid.
1 Ibid.

system was promoted for the categolical development of human being from the stage of laity to the learned one and proper function of society with creation of professional classes producers, maketers, defence personells and Visionary perisons as per their natural traits and personality types. Later on this Varṇa system was replaced by caste system in Indian Society. The real causes of suffering was explained away by the concepts of *Karma*. It made people active and awakened generating social consciousness to the extent possible under the socio-historical conditions.

APPENDIX – I
LIST OF HERMITAGES OCCURRING IN VARIOUS WORKS

Hermitages	Rāmāyaṇa	Mahābhārata	Buddhist Literature	Purāṇas	Kalidasa	Bhavabhūti Bāṇa Mis-cellaneous
Aditi Kuṇḍa	-	X	-	X	-	-
Agastya	X	X	-	-	X	X
Agastya's brother	X	-	-	-	-	-
Ajapālanigrodha	-	-	X	-	-	-
Anaṅgdeva	X	-	-	-	-	-
Arbunda	-	-	-	-	-	X
Aśoka	-	-	X	-	-	-
Atri	X	-	-	-	-	
Aurva	-	-	-	X	-	-
Bahudā	-	X	-	X	-	-
Baka	-	X	-	-	-	-
Bhārgava	-	X	-	-	-	-
Bhāradvāja	X	-	-	-	-	-
Bhairavāchārya	-	-	-	-	-	X
Bhṛgu	-	X	-	-	-	-
Bodhisattva	-	-	X	-	-	-
Cyavana	-	X	-	-	-	X
Dadhīcha	-	X	-	-	-	-
Dālbhya	X	-	-	-	-	X
Daṇḍaka Forest	X	-	-	-	-	-
Devasama	-	X	-	-	-	-
Dhaumya	-	X	-	-	-	-
Divākaramitra	-	-	-	-	-	X
Droṇa	-	X	-	-	-	-
Durvāsa	-	-	-	X	-	-
Dvaitavana	-	X	-	-	-	
Gālava	-	-	-	X	-	-
Gautama	X	-	-	-	-	-
Gautama Rahugana	-	-	-	-	-	X
Gautama Sāradvat	-	X	-	-	-	-
Hidimbi	-	X	-	-	-	-
Jābāli	-	-	-	-	-	X
Jamadagni	-	X	-	-	-	-
Jahnu	-	-	-	-	-	X
Janasthana Forest	X	-	-	-	-	
Jayasena	-	-	-	-	-	X
Kāmyaka	-	X	-	-	-	-
Kāṇva	-	X	-	X	X	X
Kapila	-	-	-	X	-	-
Kardama	-	-	-	X	-	-

Hermitages	**Rāmāyaṇa**	**Mahābhārata**	**Buddhist Literature**	**Purāṇas**	**Kalidasa**	**Bhavabhūti Bāṇa Mis-cellaneous**
KukkuRāma	-	-	-	-	-	X
Lahore	-	-	-	-	-	X
Mārkaṇḍeya	-	X	-	X	-	-
Mataṅga	X	-	-	-	-	X
Nara and Nārāyaṇa	-	X	-	-	-	-
Niśakara	X	-	-	-	-	-
Pāṇḍu	-	X	-	-	-	-
Pañcvaṭī	X	-	-	-	-	-
Parāsara	-	X	-	-	-	X
Raivya	-	X	-	-	-	-
Ṛṣyaśṛiṅga	X	-	-	-	-	-
Savari	X	-	-	-	-	-
Saradbāṇa	-	X	-	-	-	-
Saptajanās	X	-	-	-	-	-
Ƒamika	-	X	-	-	-	-
Sandīpani	-	-	-	X	-	-
Ƒaunaka	-	X	-	-	-	X
Śukrācārya	X	-	-	-	-	-
Śrutaśrava	-	X	-	-	-	-
Sthulasiras	-	X	-	-	-	-
Subrata	-	X	-	-	-	-
Sutighna	X	-	-	-	-	-
Ƒukra	X	-	-	-	-	-
Svarabhaṅga	X	-	-	-	X	-
Svetaketu	-	X	-	-	-	-
Triṇabindu	X	-	-	-	-	X
Uddālaka	-	X	-	-	-	-
Vālmīki	X	-	-	-	-	X
Vāman and Viśvāmitra	X	-	-	-	-	-
Vāmadeva	X	-	-	-	-	-
Vaśiṣṭha	X	X	-	-	X	-
Vṛṣaparvā	-	-	-	-	-	X
Vyāsa	-	X	-	X	-	X
Yaja and Upayaja	-	X	-	-	-	-

X stands for the occurrence of the hermitages in various works

APPENDIX - II
GEOGRAPHICAL DISTRIBUTION OF HERMITAGES

Hermitages	**Rivers**	**Lakes**	**Cities and villages**	**Forests**	**Hills**
Rāmāmaṇa					
Agastya	Sarayū and Ganges, Godāvari	-	Agasti puri, Akola, Kolhapura, Agastya Muni village	Daṇḍaka, Vindhyas	Vaidūrya Parvata, Agastya Koṭa
Agastya's brother	-	-	-	Daṇḍaka	-
Anaṅgadeva	Ganges and Sarayu	-	-	-	-
Atri	-	-	-	-	Chitra-Kūṭa
Bhāradvāja	Ganga and Yamuna	-	-	-	-
Dālbhya	Ganges	-	-	-	-
Daṇḍaka Forest	-	-	-	Daṇḍaka	-
Gautama	-	-	-	Forest near Mithilā	-
Janasthāna Forest	-	-	-	Janasthāna	-
Mātaṅga	-	-	-	Daṇḍaka	-
Niśākara	-	-	-	-	Vindhya's peak
Panchavati	Godavari	-	-	Panchvati	-
Rṣyaśriṅga	Kausīki	Rṣikanda	-	-	-
Savari	-	Pampā	-	-	-
Saptajanas	-	-	-	-	Riṣyamukha and Kiṣhkindhā
Śukra	-	-	-	-	Vindhya Saivala
Sutighna	Mandākinī	-	-	-	-
Svarabhaṅga	-	-	-	Daṇḍaka	-
Triṇabindu	-	-	-	-	Sumeru Mountain

Hermitages	Rivers	Lakes	Cities and villages	Forests	Hills
Vālmīki	Tamsā, Ganges	-	-	-	Chitrakūṭa
Vāman and Viśāmitra	Mandakini	-	-	-	Himalya between Kanchanjangha and Dhavalagiri
Vāmadeva	-	-	-	Daṇḍaka	-
Vaśiṣṭha	-	-	-	-	Mount Abu, Himalaya
MAHāBHāRATA					
Aditi Kuṇḍa	Apayā	Aditi Kuṇḍa	-	-	-
Bahudā	Bahudā	-	-	-	
Bhṛgu	Gangā and Sarayū confluence	-	-	-	
Cyavana	Vadhusara	-	-	-	-
Dadhīca	Sarasvatī	-	-	-	
Dhaumya	-	-	-	Utkochaka	-
Dvaitavana	Apagā	-	-	Dvaitavana	-
Hidimbi	-	Śālivāhana	-	-	-
Kāmyaka	Sarasvatī	-	-	Kāmyaka	-
Kaṇva	Mālinī, Chambal Narmada	-	-	-	-
Kurukshetra	Sarasvatī	-	-	Kāmyaka	-
Mārkaṇḍeya	Gomati and Ganges Sarayū and Ganges	-	-	-	-
Nara and Nārāyaṇa	Bhāgirathi	Vindhya	-	-	Kailāśa Maināka
Pāṇḍu	-	-	-	-	Himalaya
Parāśara	-	-	-	-	Badarikā
Raivya	Samanga	-	-	--	-
Śaunaka	Gomati	-	-	Naimisa	-

Hermitages	Rivers	Lakes	Cities and villages	Forests	Hills
Sthulaśiras	Samanga (Madhuvila)	-	-	-	-
Subrata	Dṛṣadvati	-	-	-	-
Vyāsa	Sarasvatī Alakanadā	-	-	Devadāru	Himalaya, Viśāla Badri Peak
Yaja and Upyaja	Yamunā and Gaṅgā	-	-	-	-
BUDDHIST LITERATURE					
Ajapal Nigrodha	-	-	-	Ajapāla Nigrodha	-
Aśoka	-	-	-	-	Himavan Mountain
Bodhisattva	-	-	-	-	Himalaya
PURĀṆAS					
Aurva	-	-	-	-	Himalaya
Durvāsā	-	-	-	-	Khallipahad (Himalayas)
Gālava	-	-	-	-	Chitrakūṭa
Kapila	Ganges	-	-	-	-
Kardama	-	-	Siddhapura	-	-
Sandīpani	-	-	Avanti	-	-
BHAVABHUTI AND BĀṆA AND MISCELLANEOUS					
Arbunda	-	Abbuya	-	-	Abu Mountain
Bhairavācārya	Sarasvatī	-	Thanesar	-	-
Divākara Mitra	-	-	-	-	Vindhya Hills
Gautama	Sadānīrā	-	-	-	-
Rahugaṇa	(Modern Gaṇḍaka)	-	--	-	-
Jahnu	-	-	Sultānganj	-	-
Jayaseṇa	-	-	-	-	Yaṣṭivana Hill
Kukkuṭarāma	-	-	Pataliputra	-	-
Vṛsparvā	-	-	-	-	Gandhamādana parvat, Rudra Himalaya, Kailāśa

APPENDIX - III

FUNCTIONAL CLASSIFICATION OF HERMITAGES

Hermitages	Spiritual (Vedic)	Military Education	Material Education	Ascetic Practices	Women Education
RAMAYANA PERIOD					
Agastya	-	x	X	x	-
Agastya's brother		-	-	x	-
Anaṅgdeva	x	-	-	x	-
Atri	-	-	-	x	-
Bhāradvāja	X	-	-	x	-
Dālbhya	-	-	-	-	-
Daṇḍaka Forest	X	-	-	x	-
Gautama	-	-	-	x	-
Janasthāna Forest	-	-	-	x	-
Mātaṅga	-	-	-	x	-
Niśākara	-	-	-	x	-
Pañchavaṭī	-	-	-	-	-
Rṣyaśṛṅga	X	-	-	x	-
Savari	-	-	-	x	X
Saptajanas	-	-	-	x	-
Śukrācārya	-	-	-	x	-
Śukra	-	-	-	-	-
Sutighna	-	-	-	x	-
Svarabhaṅga	x	-	-	x	-
Triṇabindu	X	-	-	x	-

Hermitages	Spiritual (Vedic)	Military Education	Material Education	Ascetic Practices	Women Education
Vālmīki	-	x	x	x	X
Vāman and Viśvāmitra	x	x	-	x	-
Vamadeva	-	-	-	x	-
Vaśiṣṭha	x	-	x	-	-
MAHĀBHĀRATA PERIOD					
Aditi Kuṇḍa	-	-	-	-	-
Agastya	-	-	x	x	-
Bahudā	-	-	-	-	-
Baka	X	-	-	x	
Bhārgava	-	X	-	-	-
Bhṛgu	-	-	-	x	-
Cyavana	-	-	-	x	-
Dadhīcha	X	-	-	x	
Devasama	X	-	-	-	-
Dhaumya	x	-	-	x	-
Droṇa	-	X	-	-	-
Dvaitavana	X	-	-	x	-
Gautama Sāradwat	-	X	-	-	-
Hidimbī	-	-	-	-	-
Jamadagni	X	-	-	x	-
Kāmyaka forest	X	-	-	x	-
Kaṇva	-	-	x	x	-
Kurukshetra	-	-	-	x	-
Mārkaṇḍeya	-	-	-	x	-

Hermitages	Spiritual (Vedic)	Military Education	Material Education	Ascetic Practices	Women Education
Nara and Nārāyaṇa	X	-	-	x	-
Pāṇḍu	-	X	-	x	-
Parāśara	X	-	-	x	-
Raivya	X	-	-	x	-
Saradbana	X	-	-	x	-
Samika	X	-	-	x	-
Śaunaka	-	-	x	x	-
Śrutasravā	-	-	-	x	-
Sthulaśiras	X	-	-	x	-
Subrata	-	-	-	-	
Svetaketu	-	-	-	x	-
Uddālaka	X	-	-	x	-
Vaśiṣṭha	x	-	-	-	-
Vyāsa	-	-	x	x	-
Yaja and Upyaja	x	-	-	x	-
BUDDHIST LITERATURE					
Ajapālanigrodha	-	-	-	-	-
Aśoka	-	-	-	-	-
Bodhisattva	x	-	x	--	-
PURĀṆAS					
Aditikuṇḍa	-	-	-	-	-
Aurva	-	-	-	-	-
Bahudā	-	-	-	-	-
Durvāsā	-	-	x	-	

Hermitages	Spiritual (Vedic)	Military Education	Material Education	Ascetic Practices	Women Education
Gālava	-	-	-	-	-
Kaṇva	-	-	x	x	-
Kapila	-	-	-	-	-
Kardama	-	-	-	-	-
Mārkaṇḍeya	-	-	-	x	-
Sandīpani	-	-	x	x	-
Vyāsa	-	-	x	x	-
KALIDASA PERIOD					
Agastya	-	X	-	x	-
Sutighna	-	-	-	x	-
Svarabhaṅga	x	-	-	x	-
Vaśiṣṭha	x	-	-	-	-
BHAVABHUTI, BĀṆA AND MISCELLANEOUS PERIOD					
Arbunda	-	-	-	-	-
Agastya	-	x	x	x	-
Bhairavāchārya	-	x	x	x	-
Cyavana	-	-	-	x	-
Dālbhya	-	-	-	-	
Divakaramitra	-	-	x	-	-
Gautama Rahugaṇa	-	-	-	-	-
Jābāli	-	-	-	x	-
Jahnu	-	-	-	-	-
Jayasena	-	-	x	x	-
Kaṇva	-	-	x	x	-

Hermitages	Spiritual (Vedic)	Military Education	Material Education	Ascetic Practices	Women Education
Kukkuṭ arāma	-	-	-	-	-
Lahore	x	-	-	-	-
Mātaṅga	-	-	-	x	-
Pārāśara	-	-	-	-	-
Śaunaka	-	-	x	-	
Vālmīki	-	x	x	x	x
Vṛṣarparvā	-	-	-	-	-
Vyāsa	-	-	x	x	-

'x' stands for the nature of activities in the hermitages.

APPENDIX - IV

VEDIC ṚṢIS *CONNECTED WITH THE EPIC HERMITAGES*

Agastya: Rv.vii.33, 10. *Taittirīya Saṁhita*, vii, 5, 5, 2; *Taittirīya Brāhmana*, 11, 7, 11, 1; *Maitrāyaṇi Saṁhitā*, ii. 1, 8; *Kāthaka Saṁhitā*, x.ii; *Pañcaviṁsa Brāhmaṇa*, xxi, 14,5; *Aitareya Brāhmaṇa*, v.16; *Kauśitakī Brāhmaṇa*, xxvi.9.

Atri: Av. Ii.323; iv.29,3; *Mantra Brāhmaṇa*, ii.7, 1; *Taittirīya Āranyaka*, iv.36, etc., *Bṛhadāraṇyaka Upaniṣad*, ii.2,4; *Kauśitakī Brāhmaṇa*, xxiv.3; *Aitareya Āraṇyaka*, ii.2,1; *Aitareya Brāhmaṇa*, viii.22.

Bhāradvāja: Rv. Vi.15, 3; 16, 5.33, 17, 4; 31, 4; 48, 7.13; 63, 10; 65, 6; *Sankhayana Grhyasutra*, iv. 10; *Pañcaviṁsa Brāhmaṇa*, xv. 3, 7. Av. Ii. 12, 2; iv. 29, 5; xviii. 3, 16; xix. 48, 6; *Kathaka Samhita*, xvi. 19; xx. 9; *Maitrayani Samhita*, ii.7, 19; 8.4; *Vajasaneyi samhita*, xii, 55, etc. *Aitareya Brāhmaṇa*, vi. 18; viii.3;

	Aitareya Aranyaka 1.2,2.4, 2; ii. 2, 2.4 etc. *Taittiriya Brāhmaṇa*, ii.10, 11, 13; *Kausitaki Brāhmaṇa*, xv.i; xxix. 3; xxx.9.
Bhārgava:	*Śatapatha Brāhmaṇa*, iv.1, 5, 1; *Aitareya Brāhmaṇa*, viii. 21; *Kauśitakī Brāhmaṇa,* xxii. 4. *Taittirīya Saṁhitā*, 1.8, 18, 1; *Śāṅkhāyana Āraṇyaka*, vii.15; *Praśna Upaniṣad*, i.1. etc. *Pañcaviṁsa Brāhmaṇa*, xii.2, 23; 9, 19.39 etc.
Cyavana:	*Ṛgveda*. i.116, 10; 117, 13; 118, 6; v.74, 5; vii.68, 6; 71, 5; x.39, 4. *Śatapatha Brāhmaṇa,* iv.115, 1.
Gotama:	Rv.i.62, 13; 78, 2; 84, 5; 85, 11; iv.4, 11; Av. iv.29, 6. *Śatapatha Brāhmaṇa*, i.4, 1, 10 *Bṛhadāraṇyaka Upaniṣad*, ii.2, 6; *Āśvalāyana Śrauta sūtra*, ix.5, 6; 10,8, etc.
Jamadagni:	Rv. Iii.62, 18, viii. 101, 8; ix. 62, 24; 65, 25. *Taittirīya Āraṇyaka*, iv. 36; *Mantra Brāhmaṇa*, ii.7,1; *Atharvaveda* ii.32, 3; *Taittirīya Saṁhitā*, ii.2, 12, 4; iii.1, 7, 3; 3, 5, 2; v.2, 10, 5; 4, 11,3; *Maitrāyaṇi Saṁhitā*, ii.7, 19; iv.2, 9; *Kāthaka*

Saṁhitā, xvi. 19; xx.9; *Vājasaneyī Saṁhitā*, iii.62; xiii.56. *Pañcaviṁśa Brāhmaṇa*, ix.4, 14; xiii.5, 15; xxi. 10, 5-7; xxii.7, 2; *Aitareya Brāhmaṇa*, vii. 16; *Śatapatha Brāhmaṇa*, xiii.2, 2, 14; *Bṛhadāraṇyaka Upaniṣad*, ii.2, 4; *Jaiminīya Upaniṣad Brāhmaṇa*, iii.3, 11; iv.3, 1, etc.

Kaṇva: Rv. i.36, 8.10.11.17.19; 39, 7.9; Av. iv. 37, 1; vii. 15, 1, xviii. 3, 15; *Vājasaneyī Saṁhitā*, xvii. 74; *Pañcaviṁśa Brāhmaṇa*, viii. 2, 2.ix.2,6; *Kauśitakī Brāhmaṇa*, xxviii.8; *Taittirīya Saṁhit* ⌊ v.4, 7, 5; *Kāṭhaka Saṁhitā*, xxi, 8. *Maitrāyanī Saṁhitā*; iii.3, 9; *Vatsa Kaṇva in Śaṅkhāyana Śrauta Sūtra*, xvi.11.20.

Kasyapa: Rv. ix. 114, 2; *Sāmaveda*, i.1, 2, 4, 10; 4, 2, 3, 2; Av.i. 14, 4; ii. 33, 7; iv. 20, 7; 29, 3; 37, 1; *Maitrāyaṇī Saṁhitā*, iv.2, 9; *Vājasaneyī Saṁhitā*, iii, 62; *Aitareya Brāhmaṇa*, viii. 21; *Śatapatha Brāhmaṇa* xiii. 7, 1, 15; *Bṛhadāraṇyaka Upaniṣad*; ii.2,6; *Jaiminīya Brāhmaṇa*, iv.3, 1.

Parāśara:	Rv. vii. 18, 21; *Nirukta*. vi. 36.
Uddālaka Āruṇi:	*Śatpatha Brāhmaṇa*; xi.4, 1, 2; *Gopatha Brāhmaṇa*, i.3, 6; *Bṛhadāraṇyaka Upaniṣad*, vi.1,1; *Chāndogya Upaniṣad*, v.3, 1. *Śāṅkhāyana Āraṇyaka*, xv; *Kausitakī Upaniṣad*, i.1.
Visvāmitra:	Rv. iii.33, 5; *Nirukta*, ii.24; *Jaiminīya* Up. Br., iii. 15, 1; *Aitareya Br.*, vii. 16 et. Seq.: *Śāṅkhāyana Śranta sūtra*, xv.17 et seq.; *Aitareya Āraṇyaka* ii.2, 3; *Śāṅkhāyana Āraṇyaka* i.5. *Taittirīya Saṁhitā* ii.2, 1, 2; iii, 1, 7, 3; v.2, 3, 4, etc.; *Kāthaka Saṁhitā*, xvi. 19; xx. 9; *Maitrāyanī Saṁhitā*, ii.7, 19. *Kauśitakī* Br. xv. 1; xxvi. 14; xxviii.1. 2. xxix.3. *Pañcayiṁśa Br.* xiv.3, 12; *Bṛhadāraṇyaka Upaniṣad*, ii.2, 4; Av. iv. 29, 5, etc.
Vyāsa Pārāśarya:	*Taittirīya Āraṇyaka*, i.9, 2.

BIBLIOGRAPHY AND ABBREVIATIONS

Primary Sources:

Aitareya Āraṇyaka	(Ait. Ara.)
Aitareya Brāhmaṇa	(Ait. Br.)
Atharvaveda	(A.V.)
Bhāgauata Purāṇa	(Bhag. P)
Brahmāṇḍa Purāṇa	(Brah. P)
Brahma Purāṇa	(Bra. P)
Bṛhadāraṇyaka Upaniṣad	(Bra. Up)
Bṛhat Śiva Purāṇa	(Br. Siva. P)
Bṛhat Dharma Purāṇa	(Br. Dha. P)
Chāndogya Upaniṣad	(Chan. Up.)
Dighnikāya	-----------
Hari Vaṁśa Purāṇa	(Hari.Vam.P)
Harsh Charit	-----------
Iśa Upaniṣad	(Isa. Up.)
Iśāvasyopaniṣad	-----------
Jaiminī Upaniṣad Brāhmaṇa	(Jai. Up. Br.)
Kalpsūtra	-----------
Kāthakopaniṣad	(Kath. Up.)
Kāthaka Saṁhitā	(Kath. S.)
Kathā Sarita Sāgara	(Kath. Sr. S.)
Kena Upaniṣad	(Kena. Up.)
Mahābhārata	(Mbh.)
Maitrāyanī Saṁhitā	(M.S.)

Mārkaṇḍeya Purāṇa	(Mark. P.)
Milinada Panho	(Mil. Pan.)
Muṇḍakopaniṣad	(Mu. Up.)
Padam Purāṇa	(Pad. P.)
Pañcaviṁśa Brāhmaṇa	(Pan. Br.)
Pārāśara Saṁhitā	(Para. S.)
Praśnopaniṣad	(Pr. Up.)
Ṛgveda	(RV)
Raghuvañsa	------------
Rāmāyaṇa	(Ram.)
Śatapatha Brāhmaṇa	(S. Br.)
Śiva Purāṇa	(Siva. P.)
Taittirīya Āraṇyaka	(Tai. Ar.)
Taittirīya Brāhmaṇa	(Tai. Br.)
Taittirīya Saṁhitā	(T. S.)
Taittirīya Upaniṣad	(Tait. Up.)
Uttara-Rāma-Charita	------------
Yognī Tantra	-----------

Secondary Sources:

(a) Authors and Books:

- Agrawala Vasudeva, S. (1964), *Vāmana Purāṇa - A study*, Varanasi.

- Aiyar, C. P. Rāmaswami (Introduction), (1962) *Economic Ideas of the Hindus, Cultural Heritage of India*, Vol. II, Calcutta.

- Altekar, A. S., (1957), *Education in Ancient India*, Varanasi.

- Arora, Raj Kumar, (1972), *Historical and Cultural Data from the Bhaviṣya Purāṇa*, New Delhi.

- Arya, Ravi Prakash, (1997), *Ṛgveda Saṁhita*, Delhi

- Arya, Ravi Prakash, (1998), *Rāmāyaṇa* of Vālmīki, Delhi

- Arya, Ravi Prakash, (2006), *Yogavāsiṣṭha - Maharāmāyaṇa* of Vālmīk, Delhi

- Arya, Ravi Prakash, (1999), *Sāmaveda*, Delhi

- Arya, Ravi Prakash, (1999), *Yajurveda*, Delhi

- Banerjee, A.K., (1967), *Hindu Spiritual culture*, New Delhi.

- Banerjee, S.C., (1974), *Indian Society in the Mahābhārata*, Varanasi.

- Barua, B., (1921), *A History of the Pre-Buddhistic Indian Philosophy*, Calcutta.

- Barua, D. K., (1969), *Viharas in Ancient India*, Calcutta.
- Belvalkar (Tr.) *Uttara-Rāma-Carita*
- Bahadurmal, (1956), *Indian Culture*, Hoshiarpur.
- Bhagi, M.L., *Ancient Indian Culture and Thought*, Ambala Cantt.
- Bhargava, P.L., (1971), *India in the Vedic Age*, Lucknow.
- Bokil, V.P., (1925), *The History of Education in India*, Bombay.
- Carr, E.H., (1977), *What is History*, London.
- Chakrabarti, C., (1953), *The Cultural History of Hindus*, Calcutta.
- Chakrabarti, A., (1958), *Thoughts of Indian Education*, Delhi.
- Chaitanya, K., (1977), *A New History of Sanskrit Literature*, New Delhi.
- Chakrabarti, H., (1973), *Asceticism in Ancient India*, Calcutta.
- Chenchiah, P. *et.al., Āśramas - Past and Present*, Madras.

- Cowell and Thomas, (Tr.) *Harśacarit.*
- Daftari, S.K., (1947), *The Social Institution in Ancient India*, Nagpur.
- Das, S.K., (1930), *The Educational System of Ancient Hindus*, Calcutta.
- Das, S.K., (1944), *The Economic History of Ancient India*, Calcutta.
- Dewan Bahadur K. Krishna Swami Rao, (1941), *Endowment Lectures in the University of Madras.*
- Dutt, S. Kumar, *Early Buddhist Monasticism.*
- Francis, H.T. and Thomas, E.J., (1916), *Jataka Tales*, Cambridge.
- Ghosha, R., (1977), *A Brief Survey of Ancient Sanskrit Literature*, New Delhi.
- Ghoshal, U.N., *A History of Indian Political Ideas.*
- Gordon, D.H., (1958), *The Pre-Historic Background of Indian Culture*, Bombay.
- Gupta, P.S., (1955), *Everyday Life in Ancient India*, Bombay.
- Hopkins, E.W., (1969), *The Great Epic of India*, Culcutta.

- Ike-da, D., (1976), *The Living Buddha*, New York.
- Ishwari Prasad, (1947), *History of India*, Allahabad.
- Jain, K.C., (1974), *Lord Mahavira and His Times*, Delhi.
- Jacobi, *Sacred Books of the East.*
- Kabir, H., (1961), *Indian Philosophy of Education*, Bombay.
- Kane, P.V., (1941), *History of Dharmaśāstra*, Vol.II, Part 1, Vol.V. Part II (1962) Poona.
- Keay, F.E. (1957), *Indian Education in Ancient and Later Times*, Bombay.
- Keith, A.D., (1925), *A History of Sanskrit Literature*, Vols, 2.
- Kosambi, D.D., (1970), *The Culture and Civilization of Ancient India in Historical Outline*, Delhi.
- Krishnamachariar, M., (1970), *History of Classical Sanskrit Literature*, Delhi.
- Kunhan Raja, C., (1950), *Some Aspects of Education in Ancient India*, Madras.

- Kunhan Raja, C., (1962), *Survey of Sanskrit Literature*, Bombay.
- Law, B.C., (1976), *Historical Geography of Ancient India*, Delhi.
- Macdonell, A. A., (1971), *The Vedic Mythology*, Delhi.
- Macdonell, A.R., (1928), *History of Sanskrit Literature*, London.
- Majumdar, R.C. (1922), *Corporate Life in Ancient India*, Calcutta.
- Majumdar, N.N., (1918), *A History of Education in Ancient India*, Calcutta.
- Marshall, *Mohenjodaro and Indus Civilization.*
- Maurice Phillips, (1976), *Teaching of the Vedas*, Delhi.
- Max Müller, F. (ed.) (1960), *History of Ancient Sanskrit Literature.* Volumes in the Sacred Books of the East (edited by Max Müller, F.)

Vol.I and XV. The *Upaniṣads*

Vol. II *The Sūtras of Āpastamba and Gautma* (Tr. by Buhler, J.G.)

Vol, XIV *The Dharmasūtras of Vasiṣṭha Baudhāyana*

(Tr. by Buhler, J.G.)

Vol. xii. *The Śatapatha Brāhmaṇa* (Tr. by Eggeling)

Vol, xxv. *The Law Code of Manu* (Tr.by Buhler, J.G)

Vols. Xiii, xvii, xx. Vinaya Texts (Tr. by Rhys Devids and Oldenberg)

- M. R. Singh, (1972), *A Critical study of the Geographical Data in the Earliest Purāṇas*, Calcutta.
- Metraux, G.S., (ed.)(1965), *Studies in the Cultural History of India*, Agra.
- Mirashi, V.V. and Navlekar, N.R., (1969), *Kālidāsa*, Bombay.
- Motwani, Kewal, (1958), *Manu Dharma śāstra*, Madras.
- Mookerjee, R.K., (1969), *Ancient Indian Education*, Delhi.
- Mudgal, B.S., (1960), *Political Economy in Ancient India*, Kanpur.
- Muir John (Ed.) (1872-74), *Original Sanskrit Texts*, London.

- Nalinakash, Dutta, (1960), *Early Monastic Buddhism*, Calcutta.
- Pande, G.C., (1974), *The Origins of Buddhism*, Delhi.
- Pargiter, F.E., (1969), *Mārkanḍeya Purāṇa*, Delhi.
- Pargiter, F.E., (1962), *Ancient Indian Historical Tradition*, Delhi.
- Paul, M., (1906), *A Text Book in the History of Education*, New York.
- Penzer (Tr.), *Kathā-Srita-Sāgara.*
- Pillai, G., (1960), *Traditional History of India*, Delhi.
- Prabhu, P., (1963), *Hindu Social Organisation*, Bombay.
- Pulasaker, A.D. and Keith, A.B., (1968), *Bhāṣā - A study*, New Delhi.
- Pusalkar, A.D., (1955), *The Epics and Purāṇas*, Bombay.
- Rai, B.C., *History of Indian Education*, Lucknow.
- Radha Krishnan, S., *The Hindu View of Life.*

- Radha Krishnan, S., (Introduced) (1958), *The Cultural Heritage of India*, Vol.I, Calcutta.
- Rao, C.V., Srinivasa, (1958), *Mahābhārata*, Bangalore.
- Rao, S.R., (1973), *Lothal and Indus Civilization*, Bombay.
- Rao, V.D., (1966), *Ancient Indian History and Culture*, Bombay.
- Roy, P.C., *The Mahābhārata of Krishan Dwaipayana Vyāsa*, Vols. I, II, III (II Ed.), Calcutta.
- Sarkar, S.C. (1928), *Educational Ideas and Institutions in Ancient India.*'
- Suraj Bhan, (1979), *Protohistoric Archaeology of Sarasvati Basin* (Haryana) (Unpublished), Simla.
- Savrirayan Jesudason, (1937), *Āśramas, Ancient and Modern (Their aims and ideals)*, Vellore.
- Sen, R.R., (1909), *The Triump of Vālmīki*, Chittagong.
- Sharma, D.S., (1961), *Hinduism through the Ages*, Bombay.
- Sharma, D.S., *What is Hinduism.*

- Sharma, Gyan, C., (1926), *Early Brahmanic Education*, U.S.A.
- Sharma, H.D., (1939), *History of Brahmanical Asceticism*, Vol. III, No. 4, Poona.
- Sharma, R.S., (1966), *Light on Early Indian Society and Economy*, Bombay.
- Sharma, B., (1968), *The Gurukula System of Education in India and its Application to Modern Times*, Varanasi.
- Shastri, H.P., (1962, 1969, 1959), *The Rāmāyaṇa of Vālmīki*, Vols. I, II, III, London.
- Sinha, P. N., (1950), *Bhāgavata Purāṇa*, II Ed., Madras.
- Sir, Risley, H.M., (1915), *The People of India*, London.
- Sri Aurobindo, (1948), *The Brain of India*, IV Ed.
- Srivastava, B., (1968), *Trade and Commerce in Ancient India*, Varanasi.
- Subrāmaniam, K., (1965), *Mahābhārata*, Bombay.
- Sundararāman, V.R., (1969), *Fifty Hindu Scriptural Tales*, Madras.

- Tagore, R.N., (1951), *The Centre of Indian Culture.*
- Tagore, r.N., (1961), *Towards Universal Man*, New Delhi.
- Thibaut, G. (Introduction), *Sacred Books of the East.*
- Thomas, F.W., *Ancient India.*
- Vaidya, C.V., *History of Medieval Hindu India.*
- Veda Mitra, (1967), *Education in Ancient India*, New Delhi.
- Venkataswara, S.V., *Indian Culture Through The Ages*, Vol.I.
- Vikram Singh, (1967), *Glimpses of Indian Culture*, Allahabad.
- Vyas, S.N., (1967), *India at the Rāmāyaṇa Age*, New Delhi.
- Winternitz, *History of Indian Literature*, Vols. 3.
- Yadav, K.C., (Ed.) (1968), *Haryana Studies in History and* Culture.
- (b) *Journals*

- *Journal of Asiatic Society of Bengal* (JASB)
- *Journal of Cultural Forum*, New Delhi.
- *Journal of the Ganga Nath Jha Research Institute*, Allahabad.
- *Journal of Indo Asian Culture*, New Delhi.
- *Prāchya-Pratibhā*, Bhopal.
- *Prabuddha Bharata*, Calcutta.
- *Purāṇa*, Varanasi.
- *Journal of the Royal Asiatic Society* (JRAS)
- *Vedic Science (Journal of Indian Foundtion for Vedic Science).*
- (c) *Dictionary and Encyclopaedia.*
- Apte, V.S., (1957), *Sanskrit English Dictionary*, Part I, Poona.
- Dey, N.L., (1971), *Geographical Dictionary of Ancient and Medieval India*, Delhi.
- Sharma, J.S., (1972), *The National Geographical Dictionary of India*, New Delhi.
- William's Monier, (1976), *Sanskrit English Dictionary.*

- Bajpai, R.D. et. al. (ed.), *The Geographical Encyclopaedia of Ancient and Medieval India*, Part I, Varanasi.
- Hasting's *Encyclopaedia of Religion and Ethics*
- (d) *Gazetteer:*
- Rai Bareli District Gazetteer bu Nevil. Naidia Gazetteer (Bengal District Gazetteer No.24).
- (e) *Research Papers:*
- Chaudhury, Bhabes Chandra; *Taksasila.* The Ancient Seat of Learning, *Journal of the Ganga Nath Jha Research Institute*, Allahabad. Vol. XIX, Pts. 1-4 (Nov., 1962 - Aug., 1963) , pp.102-13
- Lal, B.B and Thapar, B/K. (1967) '*Excavation at Kalibanga'*, New Light on the Indus Civilization, *Cultural Forum*, 9(4).
- Pandit, M.P. '*Guru Śisya Tradition'*, *Prabuddha Bhārata*, Calcutta, Vol. LXVIII, No.7 (July, 1963), pp.387-393.
- Pandey, Rajendra. '*University Education in Ancient India*', *Indo-Asian Culture,* New Delhi, Vol.XV, No.3 (July, 1966), pp.223-27.

- Purāṇa Bulletin of the Department - All India Kasi Raja Trust, Varanasi, Vol.I, No.2. (July 1959). Vol. VIII, No.I, (1966), VolX, No.2 (1968), Vol.XIV, No.1 (1972).

- Rao, M.H. '*Origin of Tapovanas*' in *Prācya Pratibhā*, Vol.VI, No.1,pp.9-14.

- Sarkar, Bhupendra Nath'*Ancient Indian Educaion*' *Cultural Forum*, New Delhi, Vol.VII, No.3 (April, 1965), pp.44-49.